INFERNO

―――•―――

READER'S GUIDE

BOOK ONE OF THE DIVINE COMEDY

INFERNO
DANTE ALIGHIERI

Translated by Joe Carlson

READER'S GUIDE

Also in this series:

Inferno: Book One of the Divine Comedy, by Dante Alighieri, translated by Joe Carlson
Purgatorio: Book Two of the Divine Comedy, by Dante Alighieri, translated by Joe Carlson
Purgatorio: Reader's Guide, by Joe Carlson
Paradiso: Book Three of the Divine Comedy, by Dante Alighieri, translated by Joe Carlson
Paradiso: Reader's Guide, by Joe Carlson

Inferno: Reader's Guide, by Joe Carlson

First Edition

Copyright © 2022 by Joe Carlson

Published by Roman Roads Press
Moscow, Idaho
RomanRoadsPress.com

General Editor: Daniel Foucachon
Cover Design: Joey Nance
Interior Layout: Carissa Hale

All rights reserved. No part of this publication may be reproduced, stored in a retrieval system, or transmitted in any form by any means, electronic, mechanical, photocopy, recording, or otherwise, without prior permission of the publisher, except as provided by the USA copyright law.

Licensing and permissions: info@romanroadspress.com

Inferno, Reader's Guide, by Joe Carlson
Roman Roads Press / Roman Roads Classics

ISBN: 978-1-944482-66-4

Version 2.0.0 January 2024

For the wrath of God is revealed from heaven against all ungodliness and unrighteousness of men, who suppress the truth in unrighteousness, because what may be known of God is manifest in them, for God has shown it to them. For since the creation of the world His invisible attributes are clearly seen, being understood by the things that are made, even His eternal power and Godhead, so that they are without excuse, because, although they knew God, they did not glorify Him as God, nor were thankful, but became futile in their thoughts, and their foolish hearts were darkened. Professing to be wise, they became fools, and changed the glory of the incorruptible God into an image made like corruptible man—and birds and four-footed animals and creeping things.

Therefore God also gave them up to uncleanness, in the lusts of their hearts, to dishonor their bodies among themselves, who exchanged the truth of God for the lie, and worshiped and served the creature rather than the Creator, who is blessed forever. Amen.

For this reason God gave them up to vile passions. For even their women exchanged the natural use for what is against nature. Likewise also the men, leaving the natural use of the woman, burned in their lust for one another, men with men committing what is shameful, and receiving in themselves the penalty of their error which was due. And even as they did not like to retain God in their knowledge, God gave them over to a debased mind, to do those things which are not fitting; being filled with all unrighteousness, sexual immorality, wickedness, covetousness, maliciousness; full of envy, murder, strife, deceit, evil-mindedness; they are whisperers, backbiters, haters of God, violent, proud, boasters, inventors of evil things, disobedient to parents, undiscerning, untrustworthy, unloving, unforgiving, unmerciful; who, knowing the righteous judgment of God, that those who practice such things are deserving of death, not only do the same but also approve of those who practice them.

~Romans 1:18–32

Dante Alighieri (1265–1321)

CONTENTS

Dante's Universe	x
The Circles of Hell	xi
Acknowledgements	xiii
Introduction	xv
Into the Boat	xv
What is Going On?	xvii
What is a Comedy?	xx
Two Dantes	xxi
Church and State	xxii
Florentines, Ghibellines, and Guelphs, O my!	xxvi
Contrapasso	xxviii
Angels and Appetites	xxx
Chart for *Inferno* and *Purgatorio*	xxxiii
Chart for *Paradiso*	xxxv
Inferno: Reader's Guide	1
Canto I: The Dark Wood	3
Canto II: Dante and Virgil	9
Canto III: Neutrals and the Acheron	17
Canto IV: Virtuous Pagans	23

Canto V: Lustful	31
Canto VI: Gluttons	41
Canto VII: Avaricious and Wrathful	47
Canto VIII: The Gates of Dis	55
Canto IX: The Gates of Dis	63
Canto X: Heresiarchs	69
Canto XI: Discourse on the Structure of Hell	77
Canto XII: Tyrants and Robbers	85
Canto XIII: Suicides and Squanderers	93
Canto XIV: Blasphemers, Sodomites, and Usurers	99
Canto XV: Blasphemers, Sodomites, and Usurers	105
Canto XVI: Blasphemers, Sodomites, and Usurers	115
Canto XVII: Blasphemers, Sodomites, and Usurers	123
Canto XVIII: Seducers and Flatterers	129
Canto XIX: Simonists	137
Canto XX: Soothsayers and Magicians	147
Canto XXI: Barrators	155
Canto XXII: Barrators	161
Canto XXIII: Hypocrites	167
Canto XXIV: Thieves	175

Canto XXV: Thieves	183
Canto XXVI: False Counselors	189
Canto XXVII: False Counselors	197
Canto XXVIII: Schismatics	205
Canto XXIX: Falsifiers	215
Canto XXX: Falsifiers	221
Canto XXXI: The Ring of Giants	229
Canto XXXII: Caina and Antenora	237
Canto XXXIII: Antenora and Ptolomea	245
Canto XXXIV: Judecca	255

Dante's Universe

The Circles of Hell

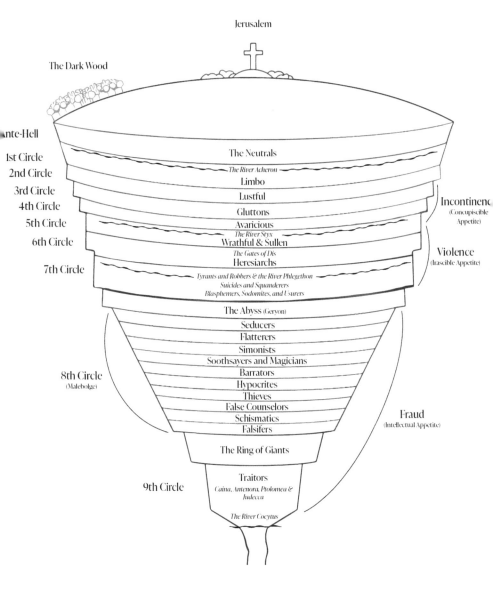

ACKNOWLEDGEMENTS

Give thanks! Give thanks!
~ Beatrice

T hank you, dear reader, whoever you are! I appreciate you allowing me to share with you those things about the *Comedy* that I find tremendously helpful and encouraging. I pray the time you spend here will be worth your while. Before you go further, you need to know that all the textual notes presented in this volume would not be possible without Charles S. Singleton's magnificent commentary on the Italian text. All of the references to the works of Virgil, Ovid, Statius, Lucan, and other authors, as well as the historical context of names and events, are straight from his notes. My debt to his immense scholarship is too great to enumerate. And so I state it here at the very beginning, before you have the chance to think I am smarter than I really am. The commentaries of H. F. Tozer, Durling and Martinez, and Robert Hollendar, were also of great help, though I turned to their notes less often than I did to those of Singleton.

Much gratitude is due to those who helped bring this to the finish line. Many thanks to Trudy Carlson for reading over the manuscript and offering suggestions. (Thanks Mom!)

Many thanks to Daniel Foucachon and the team at Roman Roads Press for their support and enthusiasm. Another special shout out to Carissa Hale for catching typos and making it all look so good. As well as to Joey Nance, again, for the beautiful cover art. And finally, this whole project would not exist without the support and encouragement of my faithful, loving wife. Her selfless gift of space and time to read and write are the foundation on which this work rests. Her husband rises up, calls her blessed, and praises her (Proverbs 31:28).

INTRODUCTION

Into the Boat

Chances are good you are reading this introduction only because you have made it partway through the *Comedy*, and are completely lost. It's okay. You are not the first; nor will you be the last. I would venture to guess that no one reading the early fourteenth-century Christian epic for the first time has a complete grasp on what is going on. I know I didn't. I hadn't the foggiest. What I did know was this: I was standing before an exceptional and momentous work of art, and if I put it down and walked away, content in my misjudgments and ignorance, I would in some way be the poorer for it. Sometimes you watch a movie, or read a novel, or consider a painting, and are struck by something indefinable, some deep conviction untranslatable into words. You know you have witnessed something true, something profoundly beautiful, but you cannot articulate what it is. That was my experience with Dante's *Comedy*. To change the metaphor, it was the same as walking into a restaurant and being delightfully tortured with the aromas of something delicious without knowing what it was. All I knew was I had to stay and ask the waiter; I had to be patient, and trust the chef. Even when the dish came, it was a goodness I tasted before I understood. However, with repeat visits, while the delight of the flavors has not in any way diminished, the understanding has grown.

    I trust it will be the same with you. The fact that you are reading prefatory material shows that you have some interest in understanding what you are tasting, some desire to have defined and articulated what it is you are reading. While I cannot fully unpack everything for you (I'm still waiting for someone to do that for me), I believe I can at least share with you some of the big ticket items that will give you some helpful context. To crowd these opening paragraphs with yet another metaphor, I want to help give you your sea legs. Stepping out of the modern, secular era and into a medieval Christian one is akin to stepping down from a dock into the middle of a little boat. If you are not careful, and don't keep your wits about you, it would be easy to fall into the water and become discouraged from ever trying to get back into the boat again. But giving up the boat means giving up the water, the voyage, the experience, and the beauty. I want to help you into the boat. Believe me, it will be worth your while.

    To do that I want to briefly unpack a number of key topics that will help orient us as we work through the various cantos together. The guides themselves contain helpful summaries of each canto, notes on interesting or obscure words or phrases, and analyses in which I discuss a theme from each canto that interests me and that I find relevant to living as human beings today. To this I have added a handful of discussion questions which are meant to push your consideration of the canto into the corners. What I want to do for the rest of this introduction is consider a few broader points that will provide a foundation for understanding the whole. With that, let's get into the boat.

INTRODUCTION

What is Going On?

Dante finished his *Comedy* (it was only called the *Divine Comedy* after his death) in 1320. He dedicated the final volume, *Paradiso*, to his friend and benefactor, the "magnificent and most victorious Lord, the Lord Can Grande della Scala." In a famous letter written to his patron, Dante acknowledges the helpfulness of introductions. He says,

> If any one, therefore, is desirous of offering any sort of introduction to part of a work, it behooves him to furnish some notion of the whole of which it is a part. Wherefore I, too, being desirous of offering something by way of introduction to the above-mentioned part of the whole *Comedy*, thought it incumbent on me in the first place to say something concerning the work as a whole, in order that access to the part might be the easier and the more perfect.[1]

He goes on to describe his great poem as "polysemous," a work with multiple meanings, or multiple layers of interpretation. These include the literal, the allegorical, the moral, and the anagogical, or eschatological. Students of medieval theology will recognize here the *quadriga*, the fourfold method of interpretation. In his letter, however, he only touches on the literal and the allegorical, inferring that the moral and anagogical follow from and are wrapped up in the allegorical. He says:

> The subject, then, of the whole work, taken in the literal sense only, is the state of souls after death, pure and

---

1 Dante Alighieri, *The Letters of Dante*, trans. Paget Toynbee (Oxford: Oxford University Press, 1966), 198.

simple. For on and about that the argument of the whole work turns. If, however, the work be regarded from the allegorical point of view, the subject is man according as by his merits or demerits in the exercise of his free will he is deserving of reward or punishment by justice.[2]

The structure of the poem depends on the first meaning; it is the literal sense of the afterlife that gives movement and direction to the whole work. Without the context of the three stages, the "argument of the whole" has no foundation. But the "argument of the whole" also needs to be understood allegorically if the whole is to be in any way beneficial to the reader. Put more simply, while Dante uses the afterlife to stage his drama, the deeper purpose is to demonstrate the soul's journey, either to or away from God. Essentially, the *Comedy* is a travel guide, walking us through a deeper understanding and hatred of sin (*Inferno*), a practical guide to sanctification (*Purgatorio*), and the true nature and source of holiness and gratitude (*Paradiso*). Throughout, Dante offers us an imaginative landscape of human affections, both in their corrupted, self-oriented state, and as they are when rightly ordered toward God.

If you are, like me, an evangelical protestant, the words "merits…free will…rewards" from the above quote will likely freak you out. Don't worry. These guides will work through all the various issues that present themselves. There certainly are theological elements of the *Comedy* that, as a son of the Reformation, I would express differently, or flat out disagree with—I would want to shy away from prayers for the dead, for instance. But I would suggest that there are not as many problematic passages as you might suppose. Part of the ten-

---

[2] Dante, *Letters*, 200.

sion comes from a difference between moderns and medievals in how we talk about various Biblical truths; and part comes from what I believe is a mistaking the literal meaning for the allegorical. I am convinced that Dante was more interested, for instance, in prayers offered for those being sanctified here and now in this life (the allegorical interpretation) than for those who have already died (the literal interpretation). He likely did hold to that doctrine as a Christian of the thirteenth and fourteenth centuries, but the specific teaching concerning praying already dead souls into Heaven is not necessary to the deeper meaning of the poem. *Purgatorio* was written for our benefit, for those of us who are still alive and reading the poem. Thus its lessons are meant to be translated and applied to our own journey toward God. The rehabituation that defines that canticle, therefore, is the rehabituation of sanctification, the sanctification of souls already purchased and redeemed by the blood of Christ. This, and other topics like it, will be discussed in more detail in the cantos where they come up, but hopefully you get my point. There is a deeper significance to the poem, a deeper significance Dante himself alerts us to, than the doctrines specific and local to his particular time and place—doctrines which we may or may not agree with when considered in isolation.

In short, there is much that non-medieval, evangelical protestants have to learn from this great work, if only we will submit ourselves to the poem, and show the courtesy and charity our brother in the Lord deserves. At the heart of the poem is a rich and profound understanding of who man is and what man is for. It is a poem that answers the fundamental questions of ultimate meaning and purpose, of existence itself. And it does so in a way that will rekindle a dormant, if not entirely extinguished, flame of transcendent wonder. It offers us the opportunity to experience a re-enchantment of the world, in which the whole created world is again understood to be a window into the goodness and faithfulness of the Creator, through which the Spirit is drawing us closer to Christ.

What is a Comedy?

A number of people are confused by the term *comedy*. Is this a rom-com? a slap-stick? Is it supposed to make us laugh? What should you expect? Well, people have been asking that for 700 years. In that same letter to Can Grande, Dante explains why he calls it a comedy. He looks back to two classical senses of the word: 1) the reversal of fortune from bad to good, and 2) a style that is able to be understood by the uneducated. He says,

> And from this it is clear that the present work is to be described as a comedy. For if we consider the subject-matter, at the beginning it is horrible and foul, as being *Hell*; but at the close it is happy, desirable, and pleasing, as being *Paradise*. As regards the style of language, the style is unstudied and lowly, as being in the vulgar tongue, in which even women-folk hold their talk. And hence it is evident why the work is called a comedy.[3]

There are certainly moments of laughter, even in Hell; there are instances of sarcasm and farce, and even puns. But those are just a few of the threads that make up the larger tapestry that is Dante's *Comedy*.

---

3   Dante, *Letters*, 201.

INTRODUCTION

Two Dantes

One of the things that becomes clear fairly soon is the difference between Dante the poet and Dante the pilgrim. This also presents confusion to the beginning reader. Dante wrote the poem, but Dante is also the main character of the poem. Dante the poet knows the whole trajectory of the poem, whereas Dante the pilgrim is walking through the story, one episode at a time. Dante the poet speaks through the various characters, achieving a polyphony of voices and postures toward God, whereas Dante the pilgrim is interacting with each on their own terms. Finally, and perhaps most confusingly, Dante the poet makes it clear that Dante the pilgrim is not always correct in his understanding. The pilgrim asks questions and reveals assumptions that his guides, and even many of the souls he encounters, have to correct. While much could be said about this, and has, I think the main reason Dante the poet does this is to identify himself with us, identify with our own misunderstandings, our own false assumptions, and our own failures to see. In this sense Dante the poet is no different than any other teacher, who meets his students where they are, and raises them to a higher (and clearer) understanding of the subject at hand. That Dante the poet does this in such a way that we often forget about the poet, walking so closely with the pilgrim, is part of his genius.

Church and State

Another element that becomes increasingly clear as one works through the whole poem is the twin emphasis on the Church and the State. As Dante argues in *De Monarchia*, man has two ends—one temporal, one eternal. The first consists of man's happiness in this life only, whereas the second "consists in the enjoyment of the countenance of God, to which man's natural powers may not attain unless aided by divine light."[4] He goes on to argue that there are different "means" of approaching these two ends. "To the former" he states,

> We come by the teachings of philosophy, obeying them by acting in conformity with the moral and intellectual virtues; to the latter through spiritual teachings which transcend human reason, and which we obey by acting in conformity with the theological virtues, Faith, Hope, and Charity. Now the former end and means are made known to us by human reason, which the philosophers have wholly explained to us; and the latter by the Holy Spirit, which has revealed to us supernatural but essential truth through the Prophets and Sacred Writers, through Jesus Christ, the coeternal Son of God, and through His disciples. Nevertheless, human passion would cast all these behind, were not men, like horses astray in their brutishness, held to the road by bit and rein.[5]

He goes on to explain that the "bit and rein" are the twin authorities of the State (temporal) and the Church (spiritual), equally and separately authorized by God alone to per-

---

4 Dante Alighieri, *De Monarchia*, trans. Prue Shaw, III, xvi, 4.
5 Ibid., III, xvi, 5.

INTRODUCTION

form their distinct and separate functions in this world: the State to aid in man's first end, the Church to aid in his second. (In Dante's argument, the State is an idealized form of world government based on the Roman Empire, led by a benevolent emperor, in parallel with the Church and the pope. Both heads answer to Christ, who reigns supreme over both realms.) However, since even temporal, earthly happiness is ordered toward eternal, heavenly happiness, the Church holds ultimate authority over the principles by which the state governs. Therefore, as Dante concludes his treatise, "Let Caesar therefore show that reverence towards Peter which a firstborn son should show his father, so that, illumined by the light of paternal grace, he may the more effectively light up the world, over which he has been placed by Him alone who is ruler over all things spiritual and temporal."[6]

This partitioning of temporal and eternal things into two realms (not in any way to be identified with the modern dichotomy of secular and sacred) is the paradigm in which the *Comedy* is written. It is the difference between Virgil and Beatrice, natural law and divine law, classical sources and biblical sources. It would be easy for a modern to read that and see a divide between man and God, but that is not how Dante would see it. Both halves of Dante's world are beneath Him "who is ruler over all things spiritual and temporal." However, only the temporal is accessible to man apart from revelation. But that does not make the temporal any less true. Natural law, for instance, is just as much an expression of God's nature and character as divine law, only not as comprehensive nor as articulate (see Romans 1). Dante held that unbelievers had access to the truth that the book of creation revealed.

---

[6] Ibid, III, xvi, 9.

And, it turns out, that is quite a lot of truth. Creation cannot reveal how man is to be reconciled to God, but it does reveal that there is a God, that certain things are right, and certain things are wrong. There is much in Aristotle, to pick Dante's favorite philosopher, that can easily be argued from Scripture. His understanding of virtue and vice, while we might tinker with it here and there, is largely true. This is an expression of the law of God that has been written on our hearts as His image bearers.

Thus Virgil, as the representative of natural reason by common grace, is able to know a great deal about vice, about virtue, and about the nature of man. He is not always right, but neither is he always wrong. His knowledge is incomplete. He can only bring Dante part way; Only Beatrice, as the representative of perfected reason, reason born again by special grace and informed by revelation, can guide Dante to his ultimate end. Here we see the difference between this medieval separation of temporal and eternal and the modern notion of secular and sacred. For the medievals (and the ancients too), everything, both temporal and eternal, was ordered toward man's ultimate end, whether that was understood to be the Triune God or simply the Supreme Good. But for moderns, even modern Christians, things secular and things sacred have their own distinct and ultimate ends. Thus, we live in this fractured state of being where Sunday has nothing to do with Monday through Saturday; where what we do for God has little to do with what we do for ourselves. We have divided these two realities (thanks Kant!) into hermetically sealed worlds. But they are not different worlds. They are not even different realities. There is one reality, the reality that God created and sustains. It is in that one reality we live and move and receive from His hand every experience. And it is in that one reality that we make choices, choices within a temporal world that echo throughout an eternal one. This is the holistic world of Dante's *Comedy*.

To this end, the poet draws examples both from the pages of Scripture and from classical and mythological sources. His point is simple: that which is true in the world is true, whether or not it is revealed in the Bible. The Bible carries an authority that classical sources do not, but wherever truth is found, it is still God's truth. As Augustine said, "let every good and true Christian understand that wherever truth may be found, it belongs to his Master."[7] This was a principle that Dante felt deep in his bones. He saw the vast sum of human experience, recorded in history and myth, as potential depositories of truth; not that there actually was a heavenly being named Zeus, for example, but that the legends and myths surrounding Zeus actually could communicate something true about our experiences as human beings in this world. Therefore, those legends and myths existed as helpful stories to direct the imagination, as long as that strengthening of the imagination happened under the authoritative tutelage of Scripture. As Christians, and especially as protestant Christians, we need not fear these ancient stories. They are part of a whole already governed by Christ. Using the temporal things, human stories as well as nature, to point to the things eternal, is part of Dante's overarching project, and part of what makes the *Comedy* perennially relevant.

---

7   Aurelius Augustine, *On Christian Doctrine*, trans. Rev. S. D. Salmond (Edinburgh: T. & T. Clark, 1873), 55.

Florentines, Ghibellines, and Guelphs, O my!

A further source of confusion in the *Comedy* is the nature of the political rivalry between different factions within Florence specifically, and Italy in general. Far more could be said, but a basic outline of the key facts as they relate to the *Comedy*, are these. The Guelph/Ghibelline divide entered Italy sometime in the twelfth century, when Frederick I campaigned there over the course of his reign. Those who supported him came to be known as Ghibellines, those that opposed him Guelphs. This divide was an extrapolation of a pre-existing set of tensions having to do with the pope and the papal power. The Ghibellines supported Frederick in order to use him to keep the pope off their backs, whereas the Guelphs fought against Frederick because his overlordship promised to be more of a threat than the pope. This tension continued and developed, as all political factions do, in ways that went beyond the original issue of Frederick and his potential establishment or removal (depending) of their liberties. During the first half of the thirteenth century, Frederick II, the Frederick often named in the *Inferno*, took up where his grandfather left off, and continued his wars against the pope. Again, Ghibellines sided with Frederick, whereas Guelphs sided with the pope. Frederick II died in 1250, but the conflict continued.

That will serve as a brief background of the parties, at least, for our purposes here. Bringing it closer to Dante, Florence, an independent city state within the region of Tuscany, was a Guelph state. Siena, also within Tuscany, was Ghibelline. In 1260 the famous battle of Montaperti was held, which involved many of the people seen within the pages of the *Comedy*. Florence led its host of allies against Siena, with the intent of taking control. Farinata, an exiled Florentine Ghibelline, led the Sienese forces, aided by troops from King Manfred of Sicily. Though the Ghibellines were outnumbered, by almost twice as many men, they pulled off an incredible defeat of the Guelphs, though not without the help of some secret Ghibellines that initially fought within the Florentine troops (see Bocca degli Abati: *Inferno* XXXII.106). It was a defining moment, and the Guelphs returned crushed, having lost the strength of their influence in Tuscany.

Dante was born in 1265 in Florence, in the aftermath of the battle of Montaperti. He was born into a Guelph family and, after he came of age, he continued the fight for the Guelph cause. In 1289, at the battle of Campaldino, a battle in which Dante fought, the Guelphs finally regained their dominance, and were able to completely oust Ghibelline influence from Tuscany. However, this resulted in tensions and infighting within the Guelph party. One group of Guelphs (the Blacks) continued to align with the power and political influence of the pope. The other group (the Whites), resisted that papal authority over their civic affairs, especially as it was located in the notorious Pope Boniface VIII. In 1300, the Whites had control of Florence. In June of that year Dante became one of the priors that governed the city for two months. By 1302 however, the tide began to turn. With the support of Boniface, the Blacks were able to regain power in Florence, which led to the exile of several White families, and politicians, including Dante. He never saw Florence again. During his exile, Dante grew impatient with both factions, and sought to pave a new way forward. Around 1312, he wrote *De Monarchia* (referenced above), in which he argued for universal monarchy; though a universal monarchy that submitted to the spiritual authority of the pope. As I see it, he was developing an early version of what Abraham Kuyper, 600 years later, would call sphere sovereignty: lawfully ordained rulers, staying within their lawfully ordained spheres. No more popes exercising political authority, no more emperors dictating to the Church. It was an idea that got fleshed out in certain ways within the pages of the *Comedy*, as we will see.

Contrapasso

The last word of Canto XXVIII of *Inferno* is one of Dante's own making: *contrapasso*. Literally it means counter (*contra*) step (*passo*), but it is closely tied to the Latin *contrapassum*, which means retaliation. Though only appearing once in the whole *Comedy*, it is the notion that defines all the punishments in Hell, and, to a certain extent, all the modes of rehabituation of Purgatory. It is the punishment that fits the crime, or the counteraction that fits the bad habit. *Contrapasso* is the corresponding consequence in the afterlife of actions taken in this life. In Hell, *contrapasso* is the unveiling, or revealing of a person's sin, in its true nature, and then endured by the damned. Thus the schismatics are themselves ripped apart, the hypocrites walk around slowly adorned with gilded lead cloaks, the lustful are blown about by a fierce wind, the fortune-tellers walk with their heads twisted behind them. The sin for which they are being punished (and it is always a specific sin, unlike in Purgatory) now defines their pain. They are wholly given over in death to what they grasped after in life. Marc Cogan, whose most helpful book will be discussed in the next section, says this, by way of describing this concept of *contrapasso*:

> There is a powerful double sense of justice in punishing the damned by the re-enactment of their sins. First, these

sins were actions freely chosen by the souls themselves during their lives. What could be more just than to allow them to continue to practice those illusory goods (now revealed as pains) which they had preferred to the one true good...As they repeat these damnable actions, they repeatedly and justly incur the condemnation for these actions that has doomed them to their places. They become, if one can say it, more perfectly damned with every iteration of the sin that is their punishment.[8]

In Purgatory, the idea of *contrapasso* takes a slightly different form. First of all, no sins are punished in Purgatory. All punishment earned by specific sins has already been suffered on the cross by Jesus. Rather, in Purgatory, it is certain habits, divided into the categories created by the seven deadly sins, that are counter-stepped. Thus, the proud walk around with boulders tied to their backs, forcing them to humbly look to the ground; the slothful must keep sprinting around their circle; and the envious walk around blind, with their eyes sewn shut. Those being cleansed and washed in Purgatory are not suffering punishment, but rather the education of holiness. Their *contrapasso* defines for them the nature of their specific curriculum. The proud need to learn humility, the slothful need to learn attentiveness, and the envious need to learn contentment. This they do by means of transformative, repetitive action, unlearning the bad habits they had learned in life.

There is a form of *contrapasso* in Paradise as well, but it has nothing to do either with punishment or boot-camp style training regimens. In one sense (to be explained more fully in the appropriate place) the saints in Heaven equally enjoy the presence of God. But in another sense, they appear to Dante

---

[8] Marc Cogan, *The Design in the Wax* (Notre Dame: Notre Dame Press, 2007), 40.

in accordance with their capacity for blessing (more on this in the next and final point). There is no difference between the holiness of those in the sphere of the Moon, and those in the sphere of Saturn. They are equally made holy and blessed by the love and blood of Jesus. But, as we know from our own experience, there is a difference in giftings, not in value, but in scope, between believers. Jesus Himself draws attention to this as His beloved children bear fruit, some thirty, some sixty, some a hundredfold (see Matthew 13:23). This is the *contrapasso* in Paradise: as saints lived various lives of holiness, so their rewards are variously distributed in glory. In other words, their station fits their life: the intellects in the sphere of the Sun, the martyrs in the sphere of Mars, the contemplatives in the sphere of Saturn.

It is a fascinating principle to see play out in the text. And more attention will be given at various places within the summaries and analyses that follow. My advice here would be to refrain from argument with Dante until you have finished the whole work, and appreciate what he has done. Whether you agree with him concerning this schema or not, it can be a valuable literary tool that helps, at the very least, start discussions about the nature of sin, sanctification, and holy gratitude.

Angels and Appetites

I want to wrap up this introduction with a discussion of the three classical appetites, as it lies at the heart of almost everything Dante is doing in structuring and enfleshing his three realms. In what follows I am drawing heavily from Marc Cogan's tremendous book, *The Design in the Wax*, where he details to what extent Dante derived his worldview from Aristotle, Pseudo-Dionysius, and Aquinas, and to what extent he took their teachings and transformed them into something new, and something entirely his own.

Cogan notes that "all action originates in appetite."[9] We desire something and that desire inclines our will toward that something. Following Aristotle and Aquinas, Dante assumed there were three basic appetites in the soul. The first two are called "sensitive," because the objects of these appetites are only perceived by the senses. They are the concupiscible and the irascible. The concupiscible is the appetite for simple goods (or goods desirable in themselves); the irascible is the appetite for arduous goods (objects that are not desirable in themselves, usually painful and difficult, but are desirable for the sake of simple goods). However, because the senses perceive only particulars (this tree, that cat) and not universals (truth, beauty, goodness), a third appetite is necessary, the intellectual appetite, which apprehends rational goods only. The chief good of the intellect, according to Aristotle, was justice.

What does this all mean in real life? Take the world of farming as an example. Food would be considered an object of the concupiscible appetite—it is a simple pleasure that provides pleasure in itself. Farming would be an object of the irascible appetite—it is difficult and painful in itself, and yet is the means by which the simple good of food is acquired. The knowledge of just and effective farming would be an object of the intellectual appetite—that understanding is not something that can be apprehended by the senses, but only through rational thought.

For Aristotle, the habitual corruption of these appetites resulted in three kinds of vice: incontinence, or the lack of

---

9   Cogan, *The Design in the Wax*, 26

self-restraint (concupiscible); violence (irascible); and fraud (intellectual—students of the *Inferno* take note.) For the medieval Christian, the seven deadly sins were also related to the corruption of these appetites: lust, gluttony, avarice (concupiscible); wrath and sloth (irascible); envy and pride (intellectual—students of the *Purgatorio* take note). I will explain the perfected and glorified form these appetites take in *Paradiso* shortly.

This taxonomy of the soul reveals both the similarity and the vital difference between beasts and man. Both share the sensitive appetites; both are driven by hunger to do various things, some pleasurable (consumption), some arduous (gathering). But only man has been given the capacity for rational thought. It is the intellectual appetite that separates us from the beasts and identifies us as image-bearers of God. As is discussed regularly in the notes to the *Inferno*, the corruption of the intellectual appetite is more hateful, and thus deserving of greater punishment, precisely because it is this capacity for intellection and reason that identifies us with our Maker. Therefore it is more of an affront than the corruption of the other two appetites (though their corruption is equally deserving of eternal damnation). In a sense, when the sensitive appetites are corrupted and dominate the soul, a person becomes sub-human, becoming more akin to a beast. (Think of Lucy's horrible thought experiment in *Prince Caspian*, when she learns that the talking bears of Narnia can grow wild, and actually lose their ability to reason. She wonders if men back in England can do the same thing. According to the Ancients and Medievals, they can.) Here is a chart putting this all together:

INTRODUCTION

Chart for *Inferno* and *Purgatorio*

Appetite	Concupiscible	Irascible	Intellectual
Body Imagery	Gut	Heart	Mind
Goal	Simple goods	Arduous goods	Justice
Faithful Passions	Love, pleasure, delight	Righteous indignation, endurance	Non-sensitive
Selfish Passions	Lust, envy	Fear, despair, wrath	Non-sensitive
Corrupt Orientation	Excess love for good things	Deficient love for good things	Misdirected love
Categories of Sins	Incontinence	Violence	Fraud
Sinful Habits	Lust, gluttony, avarice	Wrath, sloth	Pride, envy

So what does all this have to do with angels? For the medievals, the whole of creation was a reflection of the divine nature. But this was not just a nice sentiment, captured in vague expressions. No, it was the very fabric of their reality. In fact, they created whole systems to identify just what parts of creation related to the different aspects of God's character. As odd as it may sound, the angels were a prism which refracted the simplicity of the divine nature into the manifold diversity of creation. Within Scripture, and according to the classic formulation, the Triune God is revealed to be one in substance and three in persons: Father, Son, and Holy Spirit. Each of the divine persons communicate a different aspect of the character of God in their distinct relationship to creation. But combine the different persons with one another—a triad of personal characteristics within each person of the triad—and nine orders of qualities are created. As Cogan says, "For Dante, the refraction of God's simple nature into the diversity of creation means a distribution of God's single substance into nine new substances, each reflecting a different aspect of God's nature."[10] To be crystal clear, God remains three in one, not nine in one. This was a methodology to account for attributes only, not a means of expanding the Godhead.

Following Pseudo-Dionysius's seminal work, *Celestial Hierarchies*, this initial refraction of qualities was seen in the nine orders of angels mentioned in Scriptures: Seraphim, Cherubim, Thrones, Dominions, Virtues, Powers, Principalities, Archangels, and Angels. Cogan notes, "For Dante, the angels, spheres, and planets are all mirrors that transmit, through their own individuations, evidence of different aspects of that divine nature. So also are the souls he encounters mirrors of those different aspects."[11] As an aside, this is different from the order Gregory the Great gives, a point humorously made in *Paradiso*. This order of angels allowed the medievals to more clearly articulate different aspects of the Triune nature and the relationship to creation. Thus the Seraphim exhibited traits of the Father and the Spirit while the Cherubim exhibited traits of the Father and the Son (for the full line up, see the following chart). This pairing of the persons of the Trinity with each other, produced the nine-fold structure of the angelic hierarchy, which in turn gave structure to the whole universe, and so on to the capacities and faculties of mankind

---

10 Cogan, *Design*, 181.
11 Ibid., 217.

(again, see chart below). Cogan again: "Inasmuch as the angelic hierarchy matches the order of the planetary spheres, the hierarchy of human actions determined by the operation of those spheres will in turn exactly match—in fact, it has its origin in—the angelic hierarchy."[12]

Chart for *Paradiso*

PRIMARY TRIAD (APPETITES)	SECONDARY TRIAD	ORDER OF ANGELS	HEAVENLY SPHERES	HUMAN ACTIVITY AS REPRESENTED IN *PARADISO*
Father (Concupiscible)	Spirit	Seraphim	Crystalline Sphere	Primum mobile
	Son	Cherubim	Fixed Stars	Dante's examination
	Father	Thrones	Saturn	Contemplatives
Son (Irascible)	Spirit	Dominions	Jupiter	Rulers
	Son	Virtues	Mars	Martyrs
	Father	Powers	Sun	Theologians
Spirit (Intellectual)	Spirit	Principalities	Venus	Vow-breakers
	Son	Archangels	Mercury	Honor-seekers
	Father	Angels	Moon	Inordinate Lovers

Furthermore, this breakdown became the basis for the different appetites, and their different expressions, within the soul. The first triad relating to the Father primarily (and the whole Trinity secondarily) was the origin of the concupiscible appetite; the second triad, relating to the Son, was the ori-

---

12 Ibid., 179.

gin of the irascible; the third triad, relating to the Spirit, was the origin of the intellectual. As discussed above, *Inferno* and *Purgatorio* deal with the corruption of these appetites, and the healing of that corruption, respectively. *Paradiso* shows what those appetites looked like in their uncorrupted and purified state. The lower three spheres (Moon, Mercury, and Venus), guided primarily by the attributes of the Spirit, have in common a demonstration of the perfected intellectual appetite. The middle three spheres (Sun, Mars, and Jupiter), guided primarily by the attributes of the Son, have in common a demonstration of the perfected irascible appetite. The upper three spheres (Saturn, Fixed Stars, and Crystalline Sphere), guided primarily by the attributes of the Father, have in common a demonstration of the perfected concupiscible appetite. Adding another layer to this structure, Dante places saints in the lower three spheres who in life had made intellectual choices (an act of the will) influenced by earthly concerns more than by heavenly ones. This is because the Moon, Mercury, and Venus all travel between the Earth and the Sun, and are thus within the shadow cast by the Earth. To be sure, the souls that inhabit the Sun and the spheres above are just as much sinners saved by grace as the souls in the first three spheres. Dante is using this literary structure to make multiple points all at the same time. The souls in the middle three spheres all exhibit qualities related to irascibility: endurance, hard work, struggle. Lastly, the souls in the highest spheres provide examples of the perfected concupiscible appetite.

If you are scratching your head, totally confused, wondering what in the world this has to do with anything, or why any of this is at all important, the analyses for many of the cantos of *Paradiso* will be referencing this set up, and pushing it into the corners of relevant application. This introduction simply sets the stage in order for the specific instances we see in the text to be discussed in greater detail. So to that end, keep reading.

One final note. Everything in the *Comedy* has a purpose, and everything in the *Comedy* ties together. Marc Cogan expresses this well when he says,

> Throughout the poem Dante is working to fulfill three goals simultaneously: to indicate through its incidents something of the underlying natures of sin, redemption, and blessedness; to indicate the graduated seriousness of sins and vices, and the similarly graduated levels of blessedness; and to indicate the principles by which different species of sin and vice and different kinds of blessedness are related to one another—all of this with a view to our understanding both the common origin of all actions, sinful or pious, and the sacred principles by which we distinguish and judge them. To accomplish all three goals in the events of the narrative alone is impossible. Poetic details, like all concrete particulars, are by their nature ambiguous, and at every stage we would find ourselves facing the same irreconcilable diversity of personal opinion regarding the meaning of these particulars… Knowing this, Dante relies on the structure of the poem and its parts to embody and reveal the principles that enable us to reduce this ambiguity to clarity.[13]

The ostensible purpose of these study guides is to give you a firmer grasp on the basic structure, content, and flow of the *Comedy*, equipping you with a familiarity that will inform and reward future readings. To this end, I hope these guides give you the ability to delight in the story of this magnificent

---

13 Cogan, *Design*, xx.

poem. But really, my primary purpose in what follows is to give you the tools to look through the window of creation that Dante has opened, to see and understand not just the nature of the soul, nor just the nature of creation, but the nature of God Himself. As stated in the preface to the texts themselves, my prayer is that these guides enable you, ultimately, to see and know God, revealed through the face of Jesus Christ, by the power of the Holy Spirit, to live in a state of gratitude and worship before our Maker and Redeemer, to love Him by whom you were made. I will close this the same way I closed the preface, with these all-important words from Augustine:

> [We bear the image of God not] because the mind remembers itself, and understands and loves itself; but because it can also remember, understand, and love Him by whom it was made. And in so doing it is itself made wise. But if it does not do so, even when it remembers, understands, and loves itself, then it is foolish. Let it then remember its God, after whose image it is made, and let it understand and love Him. Or to say the same thing more briefly, let it worship God, who is not made...wherefore it is written, "Behold, the worship of God, that is wisdom." And then it will be wise, not by its own light, but by participation of that supreme Light.[14]

---

14 Augustine, *De Trinitate*, trans. Arthur West Haddan (Edinburgh: T. & T. Clark, 1878), 362.

INFERNO

READER'S GUIDE

CANTO I

THE DARK WOOD

Characters

⁘ Dante, the lost pilgrim
⁘ Virgil, the guide
⁘ Three beasts: Leopard, Lion, She-Wolf

Location

⁘ A Dark Wood, the Foot of the Mountain of Delight

Summary

It is dawn, Good Friday, 1300. A pilgrim awakes from a stupor to find himself in a dark, dangerous, and savage wood—on the edge of death itself. At the end of a dark valley he finds a steep mountain, robed in the light of the sun. He tries to climb it, somehow knowing that if he can make it to the top, he will be saved. But he is blocked—first by a leopard, then by a lion, and finally by a she-wolf, traditionally interpreted respectively as lust, pride, and avarice (see Jeremiah 5:6). He is forced back into the darkness of the savage wood. At that moment a figure appears to him at a distance. Dante calls out to him and begs his assistance. It is the shade of Virgil, come for the purpose of helping Dante out of the wood and past the three beasts. To do this he must follow Virgil down through Hell and up Mount Purgatory. After this, if he wishes to complete the journey to Heaven, another must take over and guide the pilgrim through the sacred spheres to the presence of God. Dante is grateful and accepts the journey.

Notes

⁙ 1: *In the middle of the course of our life*

Dante is thirty-five years old, thirty-five being half of seventy, seventy being the biblical age of man ("three score years and ten" from Psalm 90:10). Dante was born in 1265, which is how we are able to place the fictional date of this poem at 1300. See also what Dante says in his *Convivio*:

> Death is sometimes violent or is hastened by incidental weakness; but only that which is commonly called 'natural' constitutes the limit whereof the psalmist says: 'Thou hast placed a boundary which may not be passed.' And inasmuch as the master of our life, Aristotle, was aware of this arch of which we are speaking, he seemed to maintain that our life was no other than a mounting and a descending, wherefore he says in that wherein he treats of *Youth and Age*, that youth is no other than the growing of life. It is hard to say where the highest point of this arch is, because of the inequality spoken of above; but

in the majority I take it to be somewhere between the thirtieth and the fortieth year. And I believe that in those of perfect nature it would be in the thirty-fifth year.[1]

❖ 17: *robed, by then, in the rays of the planet*

In medieval cosmology, the Sun was the fourth planet in the heavens, following the Moon, Mercury, and Venus. After the Sun came Mars, Jupiter, Saturn, and the Fixed Stars. Finally, the ninth sphere was the Crystalline Sphere, or the *Primum Mobile*. Outside that utter limit of the physical universe was the Empyrean Heaven, which was the presence of God Himself.

❖ 31–54: *But behold, near the foot of the steep slope…*

The three beasts have also been interpreted as incontinence (wolf), violence (lion), and fraud (leopard); this matches the three distinct sections of Hell. The reason to align the leopard with fraud is this: when the pilgrim meets Geryon for the first time (Canto XVI), he mentions the belt he had used to fend off the leopard. However, the wolf-as-incontinence notion is contradicted in *Purgatorio* XX, where the she-wolf is clearly linked with avarice. Another scheme would be envy (leopard), pride (lion), and avarice (wolf), as these are the three vices (or "sparks") listed by Ciacco in Canto VI as setting aflame the hearts of everyone in Florence.

❖ 73–75: *Poet I was, and sang of the just son…*

The son of Anchises is Aeneas, and the song in which he is sung is the *Aeneid*.

---

[1] Dante, *Convivio*, trans. by Philip Wicksteed (London: J. M. Dent and Co, 1903), 344.

❖ 101–111: *there will be more, until the greyhound comes...*

The greyhound is a fascinating figure. While there is no clear indication within the text who it is, there seems to be both a near and far fulfillment in mind. Soon, Dante hopes, there will be a political or military figure that would come and bring peace and righteousness back to the kingdom of Florence, and the other kingdoms within Italy, from "Feltro to Feltro" referring, possibly, to a region in the north and one in the south. The far fulfillment is, almost certainly, the second coming of Christ, pictured as the ultimate Greyhound. For Dantes hope of a temporal ruler who would reign without avarice, see his *De Monarchia*:

> Therefore since the monarch can have no occasion for greed (or in any event of all men the very least occasion), as we saw earlier, (and this is not the case with other rulers), and since it is greed alone which perverts judgment and obstructs justice, it follows that he alone, or he more than anyone else, can be well disposed to rule, since of all men he can have judgment and justice in the highest degree. These are the two chief qualities needed by the legislator and the executor of the law, as that holy king bore witness when he asked God for those things needed by the king and the king's son: "God", he said, "give your judgment to the king and your justice to the king's son."[2]

❖ 113–126: *that you follow me; I will be your guide...*

Virgil is allowed to guide Dante through Hell and through Purgatory, but not beyond. Beatrice will meet the pilgrim at the top of Mount Purgatory and take over as Dante's guide.

---

2 Dante Alighieri, *De Monarchia*, trans. Prue Shaw, I, xiii, 7.

Virgil, on account of his virtue, is able to enter Eden, a picture of man at his created best, but not further because man at his best is still not enough. He must also be buried with Christ in baptism, and raised with Him to newness of life. This lack of baptized faith in Virgil is what prohibits him from guiding others to the Emperor's city.

Analysis

In June of 1300, the historical Dante, several years before he began composing the *Comedy*, was elected to the priory of Florence. He was one of six priors that governed the city, an exalted and prestigious position. He is at the top of his game. Politically, he has made it; he has climbed the social ladder, achieved great notoriety, and has been the recipient of tremendous good fortune. It is highly interesting that this is the moment, a moment that would appear to be one of great success and achievement, that the poet Dante places himself in a dark wood, having lost "the right direction." Beneath all the gilding, all the prestige and power, it appears that he is empty, a soul fully asleep to its true purpose, wasted, wracked by avarice, in imminent danger of death. I say wracked by avarice because it is the she-wolf that gives the pilgrim the most trouble (if indeed avarice is the correct interpretation of the wolf). And not just the pilgrim, but she has ravaged all of Italy with her rapacious hunger. Italy, and not Dante alone, is in need of salvation. To that end, Virgil, full of compassion for Dante, is eager to help him out of this dangerous place, and persuades the pilgrim to follow his lead.

Discussion Questions

1. What do you think is the significance of the drama beginning on Good Friday?

2. Why might the poet have chosen avarice to be the representative sin that ultimately blocks the pilgrim from attaining salvation? Is there a connection with his election to the priory?

3. Why might the poet picture himself as utterly lost when it seems he has finally "made it"? According to the poet, which is the "real life"? The prestige and fame of the world, or the savageness and devastation of the dark wood?

4. Read Jeremiah 5:1–13. Are there parallels between Israel and Dante? If so, what are they? Why might they be important to us?

5. This is a question that can only be fully answered at the end of the poem, but why might it be necessary for the pilgrim to journey through the three realms of Hell, Purgatory, and Heaven? What can we anticipate about the lessons the pilgrim might learn?

CANTO II

DANTE AND VIRGIL

Characters

- Dante and Virgil
- Mary, Lucy, Beatrice

Location

- A Dark Wood, the Courts of Heaven

Summary

It is now the evening of Good Friday, the pilgrim's attempts to climb the mountain having taken most of the day. After agreeing to follow Virgil, Dante gets cold feet. He is not an Aeneas; He is not a Paul. He is just a Dante. How could he be so audacious as to assume the right of enjoying such a passage? However, despite appearances, this is not an act of humility. Virgil identifies Dante's real problem: he is overwhelmed with cowardice, plain and simple. Virgil encourages him by telling the story of how he, Virgil, came to be in that dark wood to help Dante in the first place. Beatrice had appeared to him in the first circle of Hell, the sphere of the virtuous pagans, and entreated him to help her friend. The Roman poet is astonished, to put it mildly, that Beatrice did not consider it beneath her to descend to this place. At his request, she explains why she is there. Mary had seen Dante's plight and asked Lucy (Dante's special saint) to alert Beatrice (Dante's special love) to the situation, which prompts her to descend to ask for Virgil's help. After Dante is sufficiently rebuked into repentance, he submits to Virgil as his lord and master and follows him on the dangerous journey.

Notes

∴ Most commentators note that the first canto serves as an introduction to the whole *Comedy*, and that this canto is the "first" of *Inferno*, with the traditional epic invocation of the muses. This allows there to be thirty-three cantos in each canticle; together with the introductory canto, that makes an even 100 total. Another theory is that Dante purposefully gives thirty-four cantos to *Inferno* because of the significance of the number thirty-three, being the number of years Christ lived. He is careful never to mention the name of Christ in Hell, as a sign of respect, and it would be consistent to make this numerological gesture as well.

∴ 13: *You have said the father of Sylvius*

Sylvius was the son of Aeneas and Lavinia, born after the events related in the *Aeneid*. For Sylvius, see the *Aeneid* VI.763–766.

CANTO II: DANTE AND VIRGIL

❖ 20: *for the Empyrean Heaven chose him*

Empyrean Heaven is the tenth heaven in the Ptolemaic cosmos, not just a place where God dwells, but the very presence of God Himself.

❖ 28: *And then, the Chosen Vessel ascended*

The Chosen Vessel was Paul, who describes his journey to the third heaven (what Dante and the other medievals assumed was the heaven of Venus) in 2 Corinthians 12:1–10.

❖ 78: *by that heaven with the slowest circles*

The heaven with the slowest circles is the sphere of the Moon; all the objects of human discontent are found under the orbit of the Moon, that is, here on Earth. As for Beatrice ("lady of virtue," line 76) being the only one who can bring mankind past the sphere of the Moon, see below.

❖ 83: *from descending below, to this center*

This center, referring to the center of the earth, is also the center of the universe. However, this was no compliment as the center of the universe was that point furthest from the joy and life of God. Thus "this center" was a fitting place for Hell to be located.

❖ 92: *such that your deep sorrow touches me not*

Concerning the question of pitying the damned, see Aquinas' *Summa Theologiae*, III, Suppl., q. 94, a. 2, resp, where he says,

> so long as sinners are in this world they are in such a state that without prejudice to the Divine justice they can be taken away from a state of unhappiness and sin to a

state of happiness. Consequently it is possible to have compassion on them both by the choice of the will—in which sense God, the angels and the blessed are said to pity them by desiring their salvation—and by passion, in which way they are pitied by the good men who are in the state of wayfarers. But in the future state it will be impossible for them to be taken away from their unhappiness: and consequently it will not be possible to pity their sufferings according to right reason. Therefore the blessed in glory will have no pity on the damned.[3]

❖ 100: *Lucy, the foe of every cruelty*

Lucy is St. Lucy, martyr of Syracuse, who stands for the grace of illumination, and is therefore also the patron saint of those who suffer from vision issues, like Dante did.

❖ 103–117: *"Beatrice," she said, "faithful praise of God…"*

For more information on Dante and Beatrice, see his *Vita Nuova*. Beatrice was an object of Dante's youthful love and inspired his early, sappy love poems; she later became a poetic figure for theology, beauty, goodness, truth, and grace. She must guide Dante to Heaven, as only grace can do. Virgil, a symbol of human reason at its apogee, is able to take the pilgrim through the vices of Hell and the virtues of Purgatory, but not the holy union with Christ only grace can achieve.

---

[3] https://www.newadvent.org/summa/5094.htm#article2

CANTO II: DANTE AND VIRGIL

Analysis

Not surprisingly, as soon as the pilgrim commits to this arduous and crazy journey through the different realms, he gets cold feet. He sets his hand to the plow, as it were, but looks back. Cowardice has gripped his heart. But is that so shocking? Especially for one who was so defeated by avarice? By self-service and self-importance? This journey is not going to be an easy one, utterly bereft of comforts and soft pleasures. The pilgrim, so recently asleep to the reality of his deadly surroundings, recognizes that whatever else this will be, it will be painful, and he is not sure he is strong enough for such an ordeal, however necessary and good. Virgil encourages him with both stern and soft words, relating the story of how the three women of heaven desire to help Dante, to nurture him out of the spiritually emaciated state he is in. Strengthened by this history, Dante is now composed and ready for the "high and savage course."

But why Virgil? Why did Beatrice send this ancient Roman poet? This is a question that has produced significant discussion, and cannot be adequately answered in this brief analysis. Nevertheless, I want to offer a few thoughts to get you going. Indications from the text would suggest that Dante highly prized the *Aeneid*. Furthermore, as the supreme poet of the Roman Empire, Virgil represents the highest authority in the limited, temporal realm. He also represents what man can achieve by common grace, apart from divine revelation. (For more context, see the block quote on page xviii of the Introduction, and the paragraph discussing Virgil on page xxii.) This gives Virgil an authority the pilgrim, at this stage of his journey, can easily recognize and submit to. But more than that, Dante is suggesting that what the soul lost in a wood needs is not a lecture, not some moralistic exhortation, but the beauty of poetry. His soul is entranced with the things of this world; he needs to be captivated by a beauty bolder and more intense than anything the world can offer. Poetry stands for such beauty, and Virgil for such poetry. However, Virgil only represents the making of such beauty (see his *Aeneid*). He is a signpost pointing the way to something, and someone, greater than himself. Beatrice, as symbol of divine grace, will come as the living embodiment of that beauty, a beauty that will be strong enough to raise the pilgrim's eyes from things made and temporal, to that which is unmade and eternal.

CANTO II: DANTE AND VIRGIL

Discussion Questions

1. Why does Dante compare himself (albeit unfavorably) to Aeneas and Paul? What about those two figures is relevant to Dante's journey here?

2. Consider the contrast between the "suspended" shades in Hell and the overpowering brightness of Beatrice. Why might Virgil say he "urged her to command" (line 54)?

3. How is it that through Beatrice mankind might be lifted out of that short-sighted and misplaced contentment that defines the smallest and slowest sphere (lines 76–78)? What might the poet be saying about what Beatrice represents?

CANTO III

NEUTRALS AND THE ACHERON

Characters

- Dante and Virgil
- The base neutrals, Pope Celestine V, Charon, the damned

Location

- The Gates of Hell to the River Acheron

Summary

Having submitted to Virgil, our pilgrim is guided through the gates of Hell. An inscription over the gates tells of their creation and their purpose, and he is again terrified. Virgil encourages him, reminding him of what they are there to accomplish. This is the realm of those who have "lost the good of the intellect," that is, the good of knowing and seeing God. Immediately the pilgrim is confronted with the sound of weeping and wailing coming across the dark air. The sound is coming from the neutrals, scorned by both

Heaven and Hell, having lived neither "with infamy nor with praise." They are eternally blown about like grains of sand in a whirlwind, tormented by flies and wasps. Discovering who these are, the pilgrim spies one he thinks he knows. Though unnamed, it is likely Pope Celestine V, whose abdication after only five months allowed the mantle to pass to Boniface VIII, whose actions, regarding Florence in particular, led to Dante the poet's exile. Further on, the pilgrim sees the great river Acheron, where Charon the ferryman leads the damned into Hell proper. Crowds gather at the shore, waiting to be taken across; they are full of hatred for everything, eager to cross over to the land of eternal pain. Virgil explains that divine justice spurs them on, their fear turning into desire. Despite the waiting torments, they are where they want to be. Overcome by the sights and sounds, Dante falls in a dead swoon.

Notes

∴ 9: *Abandon all hope, you who enter here*

Famous words from over the gate of Hell. This is the place where there is no hope of escape, no hope of relief, no hope of change, no hope of redemption. It is a place made by Divine Might, Supreme Wisdom, Primal Love (notice the trinitarian formulation point to the Father, Son, and Holy Spirit). Power orders creation according to the eternal law; Wisdom determines fair and just consequences to actions; Love for goodness necessarily means the full rejection and hatred of the distortion of that goodness. Thus eternal justice is a vindication of righteousness.

❖ 18: *"who have lost the good of the intellect"*

The "good" of the intellect is truth, but specifically the Supreme Truth, that is, God Himself. It is the knowledge of God that is denied the damned in Hell. For the identification of truth as the "good of the intellect," see the *Convivio*, where Datne says,

> by the habit of [the sciences] we can speculate concerning the truth, which is our distinguishing perfection, as saith the Philosopher in the sixth of the Ethics [see Aristotle's *Nicomachean Ethics* VI, 2, 1139a], when he says that truth is the good of the intellect.[4]

❖ 66: *by the wasps and blowflies that were present*

Wasps and blowflies indicate how menial the sinners suffering here are.

❖ 109: *The demon Charon, eyes of living fire*

Charon is the first of a litany of classical and mythological figures, most of which are taken either from Virgil's *Aeneid*, Ovid's *Metamorphoses*, or Lucan's *Pharsalia*. For Virgil's account, see the *Aeneid* VI.298–304.

❖ 134: *which flared up in a bright vermillion light*

Take note of the uses of the word *vermillion* (*vermiglio*) that pop up throughout the *Inferno*. It is a distinct shade of red that is used in specific places. Here it is the color of the mournful flash of Hell, at which Dante swoons.

---

4 Dante, *Convivio*, 115.

Analysis

Hell is that dark country where the wicked and unrepentant sons of Adam are condemned to suffer fitting punishments. This is an idea that will be fleshed out soon enough, but Dante envisions each torment, each punishment in Hell not as the random whim of demons, or worse, a capricious God; but rather as the precise and just consequence of any given lifestyle. This means that Dante's descriptions in this first part of the *Comedy* have more to do with his understanding of what sin is (and what particular sins are) than any actual commentary on the afterlife. What we will see moving forward is the perfected nature of sin—meaning, sin completely cut off from this world full of the tempering common grace of God that disguises it. The consequences we see, in other words, reveal precisely what it means to sin in a particular way, with a particular part of the soul. For instance, the neutrals, whom Dante describes as "These wretches, [who had] never really lived" (line 64), and as those who were only ever "for themselves" (line 39), are continuously blown about in a windstorm, tormented by flies and wasps, envious of every other fate, and without hope of death. Before we assume the poet is simply wanting us to believe that there is this part in Hell (technically ante-Hell) and move on, we need to consider what he might be telling us about the nature of timid, self-serving neutrality. What does it mean to be one that is neither overtly rebellious nor in any sense faithful to God, but lives entirely for oneself? Can you picture this kind of person? He is the decent neighbor who doesn't steal things out of your shed, but neither does he live for the glory of God. He is not vicious, but neither is he interested in pursuing virtue. What kind of man is he? Dante would have us picture the reality of

CANTO III: THE NEUTRALS AND THE ACHERON

that kind of inoffensive (in any direction) lifestyle as base and hateful to God, but also too small and mean and insignificant to be allowed entrance to lower Hell. Here, rejected by both Heaven and Hell, they are punished for their unwillingness to live. In fact, the punishment itself identifies the listless nature of their life on Earth, as they are blown about like grains of sand. More of course could be said, but this gives us an introduction to the guiding principle of the *Inferno*.

Virgil leads the pilgrim to the shores of the Acheron, the first river of Hades from classical mythology. Charon, the classical figure ferries the souls across, souls that have become ravenous in their desire to enter the dark country, despite the tears and pain. This is because their souls have become the perfected version of their sinful state—divorced from the tempering grace of God in the world of the living. They are gnarled to the point of taking contemptible pleasure in their own agonizing pain, because they know they are home in an ultimate sense. This is Hell. They are "eager to pass over the stream" (line 124) because God has given them over to their own passions and lusts (Romans 1). Every bit of restraining grace has been removed. This is divine justice—the damned are what and where they want to be.

Discussion Questions

1. The gates of Hell were made by the justice of the Father, the Son, and the Holy Spirit (Divine Might, Highest Wisdom, and Primal Love respectively). How is Hell a creation of power, wisdom, and, perhaps most strangely to our ears, love?

2. Dante says that Hell existed before the creation of man (line 6). What are the implications of such a statement?

3. Why is Hell described as the place where go the souls who "have lost the good of the intellect" (line 18)?

4. Why does Dante create the class of neutrals, scorned by both Heaven and Hell?

5. Of the damned, Virgil says that divine justice spurs them, with the result that "fear turns itself into desire" (lines 125–126). Discuss.

CANTO IV

VIRTUOUS PAGANS

Characters

❖ Dante and Virgil

❖ The company of Limbo: poets and philosophers, kings and queens

Location

❖ The First Circle of Hell, aka Limbo

Summary

Our pilgrim awakes to find himself on the other side of the Acheron, on the very edge of the dark abyss. As they descend, Dante asks about the Harrowing of Hell, when Christ "led forth a train of captives" out of Sheol (the common place of the dead) and into Paradise. Thus all the saints of the Old Testament were taken up to dwell with Jesus, in the presence of God (where we will find them at the end of

Paradiso). Virgil leads Dante down into the first circle of Hell, where the inhabitants, living in a pale twilight, do not wail or scream but simply sigh for their fate of hopeless desire. These are the so-called virtuous pagans, placed here for no specific sin but rather for not being baptized into the Christian faith; if they lived before Christ and the possibility of baptism, they did not worship God rightly. These are the decent unbelievers, who have done nothing grievously wicked but pursued virtue as far as their human understanding allowed. First, Dante meets the poets Homer, Horace, Ovid, and Lucan. He is invited to join that company, along with Virgil, making the sixth. Together the company of poets walk through the noble castle, where all the souls of the virtuous pagans dwell. They live in twilit halls, surrounded by greenery and streams; it is stately, but sad. The list of inhabitants is a veritable Who's Who of ancient literature and history—philosophers, emperors, politicians, physicians, astronomers, warriors, kings, and princesses. Dante exalts in being given the opportunity to see so many famous people. As they come to the end of the path, the four other poets stay back, and Virgil leads Dante on out of the crepuscular light and into the darkness once more.

Notes

❖ 38: *they did not honor God as was His due*

See Romans 1:21, which reads, "Because that, when they knew God, they glorified him not as God, neither were thankful; but became vain in their imaginations, and their foolish heart was darkened."

CANTO IV: VIRTUOUS PAGANS

❖ 52: *I was newly come to this condition*

Virgil, dying in 19 BC had only been in this part of Hell around fifty years before Christ was crucified on the cross.

❖ 55: *He led forth the shade of our first father*

See Ephesians 4:8–10, which reads,

> Wherefore he saith, When he ascended up on high, he led captivity captive, and gave gifts unto men. (Now that he ascended, what is it but that he also descended first into the lower parts of the earth? He that descended is the same also that ascended up far above all heavens, that he might fill all things.)

❖ 73: *"O you who honor both knowledge and art"*

Knowledge and art refer to knowledge itself and the practice of that knowledge.

❖ 88–90: *"that one is Homer, the sovereign poet..."*

Homer was only known to Dante through quotations or selections translated into Latin. Horace (65 BC–8 BC) is probably most famous for his *Odes*, *Satires*, and *Ars Poetica*; Ovid (43 BC–17/18 AD) is mainly known for his *Metamorphoses*; Lucan (39-65 AD) is known for his *Pharsalia*. Dante quotes from all these authors in his *Comedy*.

❖ 123: *Caesar armed with griffin-like eyes*

A Christological reference, as the griffin (part eagle, part lion) was traditionally held as an image of the two natures of the God-Man. See the section on Church and State in the Introduction for why this is relevant.

Analysis

It is worth remembering, as it will come up again and again, that Dante's first goal is not to give us a literal and detailed taxonomy of the afterlife. The poem is a vision, the relevance of which is entirely for the living, for us, the readers of the poem. As we saw with the neutrals in the previous canto, Dante is creating situations, here in Hell, in order to demonstrate and discuss the nature of sin and the nature of justice in relation to human action. Much has been made about the virtuous pagans, but the first thing that must be remembered is that they are, in fact, in Hell. They are forever locked behind the gates which say "Abandon all hope, you that enter here"; they are among those whom Virgil just described as "no good soul"; they are those who, however virtuous they sound, "have lost the good of the intellect", that is, the ability to love and know God. In other words, they are not sinless, perfect, and righteous souls unjustly trapped in limbo because they failed to sign the right forms. No, their relative merit is entirely horizontal, not vertical. Compared to Judas Iscariot down at the very bottom (or, as we might say, Hitler), these were fairly decent chaps. They paid their taxes, mowed their neighbors' lawns, obeyed the traffic lights, gave money and cans of soup to the annual hunger drive, and took night classes to further their understanding of human virtue. They did not overindulge their appetites, they were not violent, and they never committed fraud. In many ways they were like the neutrals; what makes them different is that they actively pursued virtue. Again, horizontally, they were good people. However, they did not honor God as God, and they did not give Him thanks. And so they are among the eternally damned, without hope, having lost the good of the intellect God had

CANTO IV: VIRTUOUS PAGANS

given them expressly for the purpose of knowing and loving Him. Which is to say, in an ultimate sense, compared with the glory and virtue of Christ, they were not virtuous at all; they were just plain old pagans. Remember, they were among the damned we saw frantically crossing the Acheron, their fear turning itself into desire.

This fundamental division between a vertical reckoning and a horizontal one is something that has to be kept in mind as we travel down through the various circles of Hell. On a vertical plane, everyone here stands equally condemned, equally separated from the blessedness of the Empyrean Heaven, equally devoid of hope, from the neutrals all the way down to Satan. The many distinctions along the horizontal plane exist in the poem to unpack for us the different natures of various sins. Indulgence of the appetite is a different kind of corruption than violence or fraud. It involves a different part of the soul (according to the ancient and medieval understanding), and therefore is reckoned differently in terms of judgment. When it is said that the souls in upper Hell are less displeasing to God than the souls in lower Hell, what Dante the poet means is that there is less humanity at work in the sin; the soul has become more and more bestial, in that it subjects the will to appetite and lives like a beast, which has no will at all, but lives entirely by appetite. Thus, the lustful are less hateful to God (in this horizontal sense) than those who fraudulently betray their lords. The latter sin is a greater distortion of the image of God than the former, because it is a corruption of the will and the intellect—those aspects of the soul that more clearly exemplify the image of God. This framework gives structure to the whole of the *Comedy*. I spend time on it here so that you will have a point of reference as you go forward. There will be occasion to return to it later on.

All of this means that, whatever Dante the pilgrim in the story may be feeling, Dante the poet always has the bigger picture in view. And the two Dantes are often not in agreement (see the section on the Two Dantes in the Introduction). This means we need to be careful at all times to pay attention to what the poet is doing, even as he masterfully, and almost imperceptibly, manipulates us in order to sympathize with what the pilgrim is feeling. He does this to expose in us our own tendency to downplay certain sins, to disbelieve in the severity of sin, and therefore be dismissive of the comprehensive holiness of God. We are timid to acknowledge, as it says on the gates of Hell, that Love made this place. But a perfect love for goodness requires a perfect hatred of its corruption. This is the lesson Dante the pilgrim, and we with him, will be learning along the way.

As we journey through Hell, we will see punishments grow more severe, though not in ways we might expect. Justice is meted out on a continuum, with Limbo on one end and Lucifer at the other. All of this leaves us with some interesting questions: What makes the inhabitants of the first circle of Hell eager to embrace their fate? As the five poets embrace Dante the pilgrim, should he really feel so honored to be included in that particular troop? What should a Christian interpretation of the pagan interpretation of virtue be? Quite a bit to chew on, and we will be doing so the rest of the journey.

CANTO IV: VIRTUOUS PAGANS

Discussion Questions

1. What is the significance of the "harrowing of Hell" related here? Is there any scriptural warrant for this event? If so, where? If not, are there ways it is illuminating and helpful for us to consider?

2. Dante, with a great deal of confidence, places himself as a sixth in the company of the greatest poets of the ancient world. Is this pure bravado? Or is there more to what Dante the poet is doing here? Should he be so gratified to be numbered among these damned souls in this way?

3. The pilgrim feels tangible grief and pity for the lost souls here in limbo, to the point where we as readers are drawn to pity them too, almost as if it is not fair that these great luminaries of the ancient world are sent to hell simply because they were not baptized. But remember Virgil's (and therefore Dante's) own words—"No good soul ever passes over" the river Acheron. What does this mean for the so-called virtuous pagans? How might the poet Dante be manipulating our affections? And to what end?

CANTO V

LUSTFUL

Characters

❖ Dante and Virgil

❖ Minos, the multitude of the damned, the lustful, Francesca and Paolo

Location

❖ The Second Circle of Hell, the Circle of the Lustful

Summary

Having returned to the darkness, our pilgrim comes to the edge of eternal torment. Here is Minos, the legendary king of Crete, whom the historical Virgil likewise uses to preside over the underworld in the *Aeneid*, Book VI. He stands on the edge, taunting the damned who stand before him ready to be sentenced. Minos hears their full confession almost as if he can taste their transgression; after all, he is a "connoisseur of sin." His sentence is made clear by how many times he wraps his tail around his body—each wrap representing a subsequent circle of Hell (e.g. four wraps equals the fourth circle). Virgil leads the pilgrim past Minos, into the second circle where the lustful are punished. In death, they are thrashed and blown about in a hurricane, as they were blown about by their appetites in life. It is truly dark, and the noise of shrieks and wailings surrounds Dante and Virgil. However, it is not so dark that the pilgrim cannot distinguish various shades as all the great and tragic lovers of myth and history are cast before him: Semiramis, Dido, Cleopatra, Helen, Achilles, Paris, and Tristan, to name a few. Suddenly a pair of intertwined lovers piques the interest of the pilgrim, and he asks to speak to them. They are Francesca and Paolo, the famous pair of adulterous lovers. Francesca, who was married to Paolo's brother, tells their story and, overcome with pity, Dante again swoons and falls as one dead.

Notes

❖ 4: *Minos stands there, horrible and snarling*

For Minos' similar station as adjudicator in Virgil's underworld, see the *Aeneid* VI.432–433.

❖ 58: *She is Semiramis, of whom one reads*

Semiramis, according to legend, was an Assyrian Queen who, among other things, founded the city of Babylon. She had an insatiable lust, committing countless acts of adultery, and bedding her own son.

CANTO V: LUSTFUL

❖ 61: *The next is she who killed herself for love*

Dido, "who killed herself for love" of Aeneas, was the widow of Sichaeus; Cleopatra was mistress both to Caesar and Marc Antony; Helen, wife of Menelaus, became the mistress of Paris (also mentioned here), sparking the Trojan war.

❖ 66–67: *who fought to the final moment in love...*

Achilles, according to medieval tradition, was finally killed by being enticed into a temple with the promise of a meeting with Polyxena, to whom he was betrothed, where Paris killed him. Thus he died, fighting his last fight in love. Tristan, of Tristan and Isolde fame, was the tragic medieval lover who was killed by his uncle, the intended husband of Isolde.

❖ 106–107: *Love drew us to one death. Caina below...*

Caina is the first section of the ninth circle, where betrayers of kin are punished. Francesca and Paolo were murdered by her husband, who was Paolo's brother.

❖ 116: *Love drew us to one death. Caina below...*

Toynbee offers the following biography of Francesca:

> Francesca da Rimini, daughter of Guido Vecchio da Polenta, lord of Ravenna (d. 1310), and aunt of Guido Novello, Dante's host at Ravenna; she married (circ. 1275) Gianciotto, second son of Malatesta da Verrucchio, lord of Rimini. According to the accepted story Francesca, having been betrothed to Gianciotto for political reasons, fell in love with his younger brother Paolo, who had acted as his proxy at the betrothal, and shortly after the marriage was surprised with him by Gianciotto, who killed them both on the spot. As a matter of fact at

the time of their tragic death (which took place probably circ. 1285) Francesca had a daughter nine years old, and Paolo, who was about 40 and had been married some sixteen years, was the father of two sons.[5]

Boccaccio tells the story as well, giving even more sympathy to the star-crossed lovers. However, it is worth giving in its entirety, even with all its exaggerations:

> You must know that she was the daughter of Guido da Polenta the elder, lord of Ravenna and Cervia. A long, harsh war had raged between him and the Malatesta, lords of Rimini, when through certain intermediaries, peace was treated and concluded. To make it all the more firm, both sides were pleased to cement it with a marriage. Whereupon it was arranged that Messer Guido was to give his beautiful young daughter, called Madonna Francesca, in marriage to Gianciotto, son of Messer Malatesta. When this became known to some friends of Messer Guido, one of them said to him: "Be careful how you proceed, for if you do not take precautions, this wedding may bring scandal. You know your daughter, and how high-spirited she can be. If she sees Gianciotto before the marriage is concluded, neither you nor anyone else can make her go through with it. And so, by your leave, it seems to me that you ought to go about it in this way. Do not let Gianciotto come here to marry her, but rather one of his brothers who, as his representative, will marry her in Gianciotto's name."
>
> Gianciotto was a very capable man, and everyone expected that he would become ruler when his father died. For this reason, though he was ugly and deformed, Messer Guido wanted him rather than one of his brothers as a

---

5   Paget Toynbee, *Dante Dictionary* (Oxford: Clarendon Press, 1898), 247.

son-in-law. Recognizing that what his friend had told him was true, he secretly ordered that his advice be carried out. So that, at the agreed-upon time, Paolo, Gianciotto's brother, came to Ravenna with a full mandate to marry Francesca in Gianciotto's name.

Paolo was a handsome, pleasing, very courteous man. As he was walking together with some other gentlemen about the courtyard of Messer Guido's home, he was pointed out through a window to Madonna Francesca by a young handmaiden inside, who recognized him and said to her: "Madonna, that is the man who is to be your husband." The good woman said it in good faith. Whereupon Madonna Francesca immediately fell completely in love with him.

The deceptive marriage contract was made, and the lady went to Rimini. Nor did she become aware of the deception until the morning after the wedding day, when she saw Gianciotto getting up from beside her.

Whereupon she realized she had been fooled, and, as can well be believed, she became furious. Nor did the love she had conceived for Paolo disappear. I have never heard tell how they then got together, other than what [Dante] writes; and it is possible that it did happen that way. But I believe that that is probably a fiction constructed upon what might possibly have happened; and that the author did not know what really took place.

In any case, the feelings of Paolo and Francesca for each other were still very much alive when Gianciotto went off to some nearby town as podesta. With almost no fear of suspicion, they became intimate. But a certain servant of Gianciotto found them out, went to Gianciotto, and told him all he knew, promising to give him palpable proof should he want it. Gianciotto, completely enraged, returned secretly to Rimini. When the servant saw Paolo entering Francesca's room, he immediately went to get Gianciotto and brought him to the door of the room. Since it was bolted from within and he could not enter, he shouted to her and began to push against the door.

Paolo and Francesca recognized him immediately. Paolo thought that if he fled quickly through a trapdoor that led to a room below, he might conceal his misdeed, in whole or in part. He threw himself at it, telling the woman to go open the door. But it did not happen as he had planned. As he jumped through, a fold of the jacket he was wearing got caught on a piece of iron attached to the wood. Francesca had already opened the door for Gianciotto, thinking she would be able to make excuses, now that Paolo was gone. Whereupon Gianciotto entered and immediately noticed Paolo caught by the fold of his jacket. He ran, rapier in hand, to kill him. Seeing this, Francesca quickly ran between them, to try to prevent it; but Gianciotto had already raised his rapier, which he now brought down with all his weight behind it.

And thus happened what he would not have wanted: before reaching Paolo, the blade passed through Francesca's bosom. Gianciotto, completely beside himself because of this accident—for he loved the woman more than himself—withdrew the blade, struck Paolo again, and killed him. Leaving them both dead, he left, and returned to his duties. The next morning, amidst much weeping, the two lovers were buried in the same tomb.[6]

❖ 137: *Galeotto was the book, he wrote it*

Galeotto (Gallehault) was a guest in King Arthur's court, who became friends with Lancelot, and was instrumental in the coming together of Lancelot and Queen Guinevere.

---

[6] Charles S. Singleton, *Inferno: Commentary* (Princeton, NJ: Princeton University Press, 1989), 87-89.

CANTO V: LUSTFUL

Analysis

The second circle of Hell is reserved for those who allowed themselves to be ruled not by their reason, but by their lowest appetites, by their lusts. Technically speaking, it is the appetite of concupiscence (see the section on Angels and Appetites in the Introduction). The souls here are governed not by rationality, but by the simple lust for pleasure, most often manifested in the active pursuit of licentiousness. The souls blustered about by the winds now outwardly inhabit the nature of the inward disposition that defined them while still alive. But, however much they are blown about, they are still unwilling to admit to why they are here. They have, with all souls in Hell, lost the good of the intellect, which means they have lost the good of recognizing justice. What remains is a bent, twisted, and self-serving pseudo-rationality that eternally blames the other. Francesca blames "Love" (*amor*) for all her woes, and does so three times. It was love that made them do it, love that put them in this fix, love that is so unforgiving. Her attitude exhibits zero repentance and zero remorse, which is to be expected.

The scene between Francesca and Dante is fascinating, and has given rise to oceans of ink in commentary and discussion. What fascinates me is how much the language literally drips with sensuality and passion—both Francesca's, which we should expect, and the pilgrim's, which is highly interesting. Go back and read through the exchange (starting at line 73) through to the end, paying special attention to Dante the pilgrim's words, and the brief commentary about how he was feeling in that moment. Pay attention to the bird similes. Dante the poet is setting the scene such that the pilgrim is in complete and total sympathy with these damned souls. Without saying as much, he has taken their side, and enters into the bitterness of their fate. "O misery, / how many sweet thoughts, and how much desire / delivered them to this wretched station!" (lines 112–114). Even when he asks how they became aware of their illicit feelings, he couches it in softer and safer language: those "dubious desires" (line 120). She has won him over. He is a votary to courtly love, and stands before true lovers, jealously killed for the purity of their love.

Behold the genius of Dante the poet. In giving us such an intimate and sensual conversation, we, with the pilgrim, focus so tightly on the immediacy of the story that we forget the context. Francesca and Paolo are eternally damned by their own heinous transgression, blown about by their passions, unrepentant, completely lacking in remorse, willingly continuing forever and ever, world without end, their sinful, self-serving inversion of true love, and by extension, their utter rejection of the God who Himself is Love. In short, we are not supposed to pity the damned. And by pity I mean an emotional sympathizing with them in their pain and agony; an entering into their grievance against the laws of nature, as if they are somehow victims of anything but their own bad choices. Dante the pilgrim sees Francesca as the injured party, and the unfairness of it doubles him over in grief. The reality is, he sees her the way she wants to be seen. She is casting the story, with her and Paolo as the tragic heroes, and the pilgrim bites, and bites hard. This will be a recurring theme, and will constitute much of Dante's development in Hell. He will learn, over time, not to take the sinners' gripes at face value, but to recognize that they, having lost the good of the intellect, are not to be trusted as honest and neutral appraisers of their own stories. But that is a lesson yet to be learned here,

CANTO V: LUSTFUL

at the end of Canto V. Instead we have Dante swooning once again, this time from pity and the deep affection he feels for these suffering lovers.

Discussion Questions

1. As with Charon, Minos is taken from pagan mythology and given a place here in Dante's Hell. Why? What is Dante doing?

2. What is going on with all of the bird similes in this canto? Why might it be significant?

3. Why is a soul governed by the appetite so harmful both to itself and to others?

4. Remembering Dante's use of *contrapasso*, how does the punishment fit the crime? How is it a perfected image of the sin being punished?

5. Why is the pilgrim so filled with pity for the damned lovers? Is this a good thing? Is Dante the poet praising and holding up Dante the pilgrim as exemplary?

6. How does Francesca feel about her sin? What does she think about it?

7. What might these questions and answers reveal about the virtuous pagans of the previous canto?

CANTO VI

GLUTTONS

Characters

❖ Dante and Virgil
❖ Cerberus, the gluttonous, Ciacco

Location

❖ The Third Circle of Hell, the Circle of the Gluttons

Summary

Still confused and saddened by his conversation with Francesca, our pilgrim awakes and descends to the third circle of Hell. He and Virgil are met by the mythical Cerberus, the demon with three doglike heads. He growls at the visitors, a monstrous symbol of gluttony. Virgil quickly picks up some dirt and throws it down the three throats, which distracts Cerberus long enough for them to push past. They enter the place where the gluttonous are punished, submerged in filth and sludge. All seem to be empty shells, lying buried and indistinguishable in the muck. But one sits up and engages Dante in conversation. It is Ciacco, a Florentine, placed here by Dante for his extravagant eating habits. Dante again feels tremendous pity. He asks Ciacco what the spirit knows about their native city. Ciacco describes the coming conflict that will eventually lead to Dante's exile. Between the years of 1300 and 1302 ("within three years"), the White Guelphs (the "savage sect," Dante's own party) would defeat the Black Guelphs. But the Blacks would return with the help of Boniface VIII, who would feign neutrality ("straddle the shore"). With their help, the Whites would be placed "beneath the heavy weights" of exile or death. Dante himself would be exiled in 1302. After this, they briefly speak of other famous Florentines, who dwell further down in the abyss (we will meet Farinata in Canto X, Tegghiaio and Rusticucci in Canto XVI, and Mosco in Canto XXVIII; Arrigo is not mentioned again, but is probably with Mosco). Refusing to answer any more questions, Ciacco sinks back into the mud. Dante and Virgil move on, discussing the state of these souls after the final judgment.

Notes

∴ 13: *Cerberus, that cruel and deviant beast*
Cerberus is lifted from the *Aeneid*, Book VI.417–423.

∴ 16: *His eyes bright vermillion, beard greased and black*
Note the second instance of the adjective *vermillion*, this time describing the six bright eyes of Cerberus.

CANTO VI: GLUTTONS

❖ 52: *You citizens called me Ciacco, the pig*

Ciacco (which means "hog") is the shortened form of Giacomo, and potentially refers to Giacomo dell'Anguillaia, a Florentine poet of the thirteenth century.

❖ 61: *to the subjects of that shattered city*

For the "shattered" state of Florentine politics, see the section in the Introduction titled "Florentines, Ghibellines, and Guelphs, O my!"

❖ 69: *of one that even now straddles the shore*

This is a reference to Boniface VIII, who was instrumental in orchestrating the events that led to Dante's permanent exile in 1302, which is what Ciacco is hinting at in this passage.

❖ 95: *til the sound of the angelic trumpet*

Virgil is referring to the trumpet sound declaring the Final Judgment and the resurrection of the dead. See Matthew 24:27–31, John 5:29, and 1 Corinthians 15:51–53.

❖ 106: *He said to me, "Return to your science"*

Virgil tells Dante to go back to his "science," that is, his philosophy. In particular, Dante is to remember the Aristotelian and Thomistic teaching that the soul is not complete (perfect) without the body (see Aristotle's *De anima* II, i, 412a and Aquinas' *Summa Theologiae* I, q. 90, a. 4, resp.). In this perfected state, after the resurrection, the souls in Hell will all have their bodies. Therefore, though their punishments will not increase, their ability to feel them will. This soul/body relationship continues to be a major theme, especially when we get to *Paradiso*.

Analysis

As we saw in the introduction, the upper circles of Hell are populated by those who let their appetites rule over their reason. These are the sins of concupiscence—the controlling desire (at the expense of reason and obedience) for pleasure, be it sex (as in the previous Canto) or food (as with the gluttons). The basic Augustinian idea is this: something that in itself is morally neutral, or even a positive good (such as sex and food), becomes the object of inordinate (out of order) desire. These sinners want good things like food so much that they are willing to sacrifice everything for the sake of that one good, even their reason. In essence, they idolize that object to the point of damnation. They have traded the good of their souls for momentary pleasures, without fully enjoying them; for desired and consumed in such a sinful way, those pleasures can never satisfy. And so, their punishment is to embrace, forever, the true reality behind their sin. They must literally eat filth, drink filth, lie submerged in filth for eternity. This is the true end of their appetite. This is what all those momentary pleasures truly become in relation to the soul that seeks them for the sake of the pleasure alone. Again, there is nothing evil about the objects of pleasure, like food, in themselves. But a disordered pleasure is deceptive, misguided, and ultimately disgusting. And so, their consequence is to fill their gullets with the dirt, just as Cerberus was forced to do. They have so disregarded the rational intellect given them by God, they are given over to a union with the dirt. They are, in a sense, returned to the earth from which they were made.

It is interesting however, that instead of asking about gluttony, Dante asks about Florence, and what will happen to her in the coming years. The spirits in Hell are given some knowledge of what will happen, though in a vague way (this is explained in a later canto). Ciacco is therefore able to tell Dante what he wants to hear. Through "envy, pride, and avarice" (line 74; remember the leopard, lion, and she-wolf of Canto I), Florence has fractured into unstable parties. As men become gluttons for food, ignoring the good of the intellect, and bring upon themselves the destructive consequence of their indulgence, so too, cities become gluttons for power. In doing this they abandon the rational principle of governance, and are forced to embrace the dissolving consequences of such a move. As the gluttons in Hell are broken down and submerged in the muck, so too the city breaks down, losing the unifying elements of justice, truth, and goodness. Ciacco is Florence; and Ciacco's fate looks to be the fate of the city as well.

Discussion Questions

1. Why was Cerberus chosen as a guard for this circle? What do his appetites tell us about the sinners here?

2. Sinners in Hell willingly embrace their punishments as it is the fullest and most complete embodiment of their specific sin. What does the muck and filth in which they are submerged, blind and indistinguishable, tell us about the sin of Gluttony?

3. Why do you think the subject of Dante and Ciacco's discussion is not gluttony, but politics? What is the connection between gluttony, envy, and political maneuvering?

4. Dante pities Ciacco, and is greatly grieved to see him here, as he was previously with Francesca and Paolo. Is he right in doing so? Why or why not?

5. What do the final lines of this canto mean? What does it mean that the more perfect something becomes, the more it is able to sense good and pain? What relation does that have to the final resurrection of the good and the bad, especially with regard to the eternal, bodily judgment that will follow?

CANTO VII

AVARICIOUS AND WRATHFUL

Characters

∴ Dante and Virgil

∴ Plutus, the god of wealth

∴ The avaricious and the wrathful

Location

∴ The Fourth Circle of Hell, the Circle of the Avaricious (the spendthrifts and misers)

∴ The Fifth Circle of Hell, the Circle of the Wrathful (the brutal and the sullen)

Summary

On entering the fourth circle, the travelers are hindered by Plutus, "the great enemy" as he was called at the end of the previous canto. He is the demonic god of wealth (not to be confused with Pluto, the god of the dead), and represents the avaricious souls who are behind him as Cerberus represented the gluttons. He utters words that are untranslatable, and yet that seem to be understood by Virgil, who waves him aside, calming Dante's fears. They descend to the pit where the greedy are punished. Here are both the spendthrifts and the misers, who committed opposite though complimentary sins, both rooted in an inordinate love of money. One group loves hoarding what money buys, the other loves hoarding money itself. The consequence of their sin is to eternally roll giant boulders round and round in a circle, the spendthrifts going round in one direction, the misers in the other. At the two points of the circle where they meet, they crash into one another, accusing one another of their respective misdeeds. Dante notices that there are many clerics here, popes and cardinals, both of whom were consumed with extreme greed. The pilgrim thinks he should be able to recognize some of them, but Virgil corrects him. Here, the inordinate love of worldly goods has so marred and disfigured their souls that they have become unrecognizable. The nature of Fortune is discussed at length as they continue down to the fifth circle. Shortly after midnight, in the first moments of Holy Saturday, the travelers approach the Styx. There, the wrathful are punished by being submerged in the swamp. They too are indistinguishable from one another, their humanity effaced by their sin. Two kinds of wrath are briefly alluded to: first, the outright violence of physical brutality, and second, the bitterness of those who refused to enjoy the good things of the world. The violent bite and snarl and tear one another with their teeth. The sullen abused the kind gifts God had bestowed on them through perpetual sadness. Dante is astonished as he watches them eat the muck they are buried in. Directly after this, they come to the foot of a tower.

CANTO VII: AVARICIOUS AND WRATHFUL

Notes

❖ 12: *where Michael punished the proud treachery*

The archangel Michael fought the dragon, and cast him from Heaven, punishing the "proud treachery." See Revelation 12:7–9.

❖ 22–24: *As the wave, there above Charybdis, breaks...*

Charybdis (a whirlpool) and Scylla (first a sea monster, and later a rock), formed a famously dangerous channel, which would routinely wreck havoc on ships and sailors alike. See the *Aeneid* III.420–423.

❖ 74–76: *made the heavens and gave them conductors...*

Nine conductors, or angelic intelligences, govern the nine heavenly spheres, such that every part of every sphere has the light of God reflected through it by means of the intelligences (see the section on Angels and Appetites in the Introduction). This will be thoroughly fleshed out in *Paradiso*. See also the *Convivio*, where Dante says, "Be it known, therefore, firstly, that the movers thereof are substabces sejunct [separated] from matter, to wit, Intelligences, which are vulgarly called Angels."[7]

❖ 87: *and rules her wheel like all the lesser gods*

For the angelic intelligences being referred to as "lesser gods" see the *Convivio* again, where Dante continues:

---

7 Dante, *Convivio*, 78.

Others were there such as Plato, a man of supreme excellence, who laid down not only as many Intelligences as there are movements of heaven, but just as many as there are kinds of things as all men one kind, and all gold another kind, and all riches another, and so throughout the whole; and they would have it that as the Intelligences of the heavens are the generators of the same, each of his own, so those others were the generators of the other things, and the exemplars each one of his own kind; and Plato calls them Ideas, which is as much as to say Forms, and Universals. The Gentiles called them gods and goddesses...[8]

Analysis

It is interesting to note that both the avaricious and the wrathful pictured here in this canto are described as unrecognizable. There is something in both greed and anger that, in their ultimate expression, reduces a person's humanity, such that we cannot know who they are. Tellingly, there are no conversations with the lost here; there are no remembrances or cries for pity. Furthermore, with regard to the fourth circle, that of the avaricious, Dante says this was the circle that held the most sinners. Remember back to the image of the she-wolf in Canto I, which, representing avarice, was described as having made so many wretched, and was the destroyer of Italy. It is worth thinking about how greed (exhibited both in the spendthrifts and the misers) alienates sinners from the world and from one another. Greed, in embracing a love of self over

---

[8] Dante, *Convivio*, 78.

CANTO VII: AVARICIOUS AND WRATHFUL

everything, turns everything into an object of consumption. The greedy, whether they satisfy their concupiscence with the accumulation of mammon or simply the golden coin itself, become dismissive of the humanity of others, turning them into mere means.

That said, this circle is still in the upper regions of Hell, where the sins of incontinence, or immoderate appetites, are punished. Like the lustful and the gluttons, the avaricious here are not judged for any intellectual sin leading specifically to injustice. Rather they are punished for an abundance of uncontrolled, unmeasured appetite. It is therefore not a willful objectifying of others, but rather the inevitable result of their immoderate passion for stuff (willful dismissiveness being punished further down). This is imaged for us in the frantic necessity of forever rolling these giant boulders, unable to stop, except to hurl insults while still pressing forward. They have never been ruled by their intellect, and whatever good they did have of it in life, is now utterly gone. They are left only with their destructive passion.

The wrathful and sullen, housed in the fifth circle and within the border of one of the major divisions in the geography of hell, tell a mixed story. They are the gateway, so to speak, to the first region of lower Hell, where the sins of irascibility (or violence proper) are dealt with. Here, the wrathful and the sullen are still overcome by the incontinence that is punished in upper hell. Following Cogan's interpretation, the wrathful take pleasure in unpleasant things, and the sullen take displeasure in pleasant things. Both are overcome by their passions, both are acting purely from an incontinent appetite. There is not a direct transgression of the intellectual capacity; rather it is one of mistaken passion, though still tragic and destructive. The pilgrim will speak with one of the wrathful in the following canto, but here they are pictured as, again, consumed by their particular sins: the outwardly wrathful in eternal and violent contest with one another; the internally wrathful (the sullen) submerged in the rotting filth they had invited into their soul while alive.

Sandwiched in between these two circles is a fascinating discussion of Lady Fortune. Modern day Christians might have a tough time swallowing the descriptions of this "goddess", and for many different reasons. But starting with charity toward Dante the poet, the reader ought to lay aside any immediate repulsion to the idea, and consider the deeper reality that is being communicated. What he describes, when the trappings of classical mythology are set to one side, is the nature of Providence, and specifically the reign of Christ in this world. Lady Fortune is by no means synonymous with blank chance, let alone chaos. She is ordered, and given instructions, and rules under the sovereignty of God on High. She governs in an inscrutable manner; she judges and foresees actions and events; and acts herself with some amount of sovereignty within the lives of men. She is crucified, scorned, and mocked by those whom she blesses. But she remains above it all, unaffected by those who malign her. She is content to rule within the sphere given her by the Almighty. *Mutatis mutandis*, this is a fairly detailed description of Jesus as the crucified, risen, and ascended Lord of all History. Far from Fortune (as we might conceive of the idea) governing the lives of men, this great lady stands as a poetic image of Christ Himself, on the throne, governing all things well, even if in such a way that defies man's understanding. His ways are above our ways, after all.

There is much packed in, and much to consider in this canto. Perhaps the most interesting question is this: what do the three separate episodes (the avaricious, the discussion of Fortune, the wrathful) have to do with one another? Why did the poet place each element together, in this one canto? What is the common thread, if there is one, that runs through each? I have no definite answer, only a suggestion. Consider fallen man's response to Providence. Without faith or trust in the goodness and personal kindness of Lady Fortune (or, Christ), it seems greediness, biting, and sullenness are three very natural responses to the vicissitudes of this life. We hoard or spend on treasures and possessions against the possibility of bad fortune; we bite and devour one another when we think of ourselves as victims of bad fortune; we grow sullen in the face of genuine blessings, simply because it's not exactly what we want. Perhaps this is the final result of letting one's appetite govern in place of one's reason. Reason, if we are honest, would recognize that we can't take it with us, our own lot is not the fault of others, and that to be sullen in the face of what is good is stupid and destructive. The problem is, we are not honest. We are selfish, and our appetites demand more and more of us. If we give them free rein, they will destroy us. They will cause us to bear "within ourselves acidic fumes" even though we dwell in the "sweet air made glad by the sun" (lines 122–123).

INFERNO READER'S GUIDE

Discussion Questions

1. What role does Plutus play in setting the scene of this canto?

2. What is the unifying connection between the spendthrifts and the misers?

3. Virgil says, "Bad giving and bad holding removed them from the beautiful world…" (lines 58–59). He doesn't mean that is what killed them. They were removed from the beautiful world before their death. This "brawl" is merely the final outworking of a reality that existed in their life. What does that mean? What might that have looked like?

4. Discuss the connection between Lady Fortune and King Jesus. Why might Dante use such a metaphor (if that is in fact what he is doing, of course)? If you see no connection, discuss her presence and what else she might signify.

5. Why are both the brutal and sullen described as wrathful, or as "those who were conquered by wrath" (line 116)?

6. What are the "acidic fumes" that the sullen draw in on a fresh sunny day?

CANTO VIII

THE GATES OF DIS

Characters

∴ Dante and Virgil
∴ Phlegyas, the boatman of the Styx
∴ The wrathful Filippo Argenti
∴ The demons of Dis

Location

∴ The Fifth Circle of Hell, the Circle of the Wrathful (the brutal and the sullen)
∴ Outside the city gates of Dis

Summary

Before describing the "high tower", Dante recounts an incident that occurred before the last line of the previous canto. Standing on the far side of the Styx, they see two lights and an answering signal. At the signal comes Phlegyas, the boatman of the Styx. As Cerberus and Plutus watch over their circles, Phlegyas watches over the fifth circle. Virgil forces him to carry them across the Styx, so that they can continue their journey to the "high tower." While in the boat, one of the wrathful rises up out of the muck and asks Dante who he is. Dante does not oblige but instead curses this sinner, whom he recognizes as Filippo Argenti (a Florentine). The angered soul reaches out to do violence, but Virgil dispenses with him easily, and he returns to the muck. Virgil praises Dante's righteous indignation, after which the pilgrim asks if he can watch Argenti be devoured by the other violent souls; his wish is granted. He watches until Argenti begins tearing his own flesh with his teeth. They cross the Styx and make their way to the gates of Dis. Dante sees the host of demons on top of the gates, and hears their taunts. Virgil begs an audience, is received, and comes back angry that these demons will not obey his wish. The canto ends with the pair stalled but with hints that someone greater is coming who will open the doors for them.

Notes

⁖ 1: *I say, continuing, that long before*

With regard to the unique opening on this canto ("I say, continuing,") there is a tradition that holds the first seven cantos were written before Dante's exile in 1302, while the rest of the *Comedy*, starting here in Canto VIII, was picked up and finished between the years 1307 and 1320. It should be noted

CANTO VIII: THE GATES OF DIS

that, while Boccaccio believed this story, it is without substantial evidence.

❖ 19: *"Phlegyas, Phlegyas, you shout but empty words"*

Phlegyas burned down the temple of Apollo at Delphi after the god violated his daughter. For this act he was condemned to Tartarus. See the *Aeneid* V.618–620 and Statius' *Thebaid* I.712–715.

❖ 61: *All shouted, "At Filippo Argenti!"*

Filippo Argenti was one of the Cavicciuli branch of the Adimari family of Florence, and was a rough contemporary of Dante's. The Adimari family was especially hostile toward Dante, some going so far as to steal some of Dante's property after his exile.

❖ 68–72: *to the city bearing the name of Dis...*

Dis is pictured as a city of the Moors, or Saracens, complete with mosques. For Virgil's use of the name Dis, see *Aeneid* VI.127 and 541.

❖ 72: *vermillion most clearly, as from the fire*

Notice the third instance of the adjective *vermillion*—the hue cast by the fires of the city.

❖ 94: *Consider, reader, if I quailed at this*

Seven times throughout the *Inferno*, Dante the poet addresses his "readers," posing questions directly to us.

Analysis

Phlegyas, the boatman of the Styx, according to Greek mythology, was condemned to Tartarus (or Hell) because he was angry at Apollo and burned down his temple at Delphi. Dante continues to use classical figures as governors for each circle, figures that in some way embody the sin that is there punished. Cerberus was a gluttonous demon-dog, Plutus was the god of wealth, and here we have Phlegyas, a wrathful man condemned for his impassioned violence against the gods. Like we saw in the previous canto, it is important to remember why the wrathful are punished in upper Hell (though they are actually within the dividing line of the Styx itself). Upper Hell is where those are punished who were overcome by their passions and appetites—the gut ruling over the mind. Their sins were not calculated, in other words. They were not reasoned through, or premeditated. In this way, Dante draws an important distinction between the wrathful and the violent in the following cantos. Those punished in the following circles, as we will see, were violent in such a way that their intellect was engaged. Their violence, though often having the same effect, was a reasoned choice, more than the result of the short-tempered wrath exhibited by the people in the Styx.

People like Filippo Argenti. He suddenly rises out of the swampy Styx, like a scene out of a horror movie, and accosts the travelers in the boat. And for the first time, the pilgrim Dante does not immediately feel pity for the punished. He is learning to see sin for what it is. This is a striking moment, and one that Virgil recognizes as well. "Superior soul!" (line 44) he says, blessing Dante's mother for bringing him into this world, hugging and kissing him. These are men and women who have utterly rejected not only God and God's grace (that

CANTO VIII: THE GATES OF DIS

much we expect in Hell), but the very laws of nature as well. These are the souls of those who have rejected their own humanity, and the humanity of others. This circle, including what we saw of it in the previous canto, presents us with the clearest picture we have yet seen of the dehumanizing nature of sin. The violently wrathful are literally biting and tearing each other to pieces. And as we see here, they even start to bite and tear themselves, in utter rejection of both the image of God, and the natural human form.

The pity the pilgrim has shown up to this point for the sinners, like Francesca, betrays a misunderstanding about what is happening. Pity takes up the case of the sinner, and identifies them in some way as a victim. In pitying the sinners, Dante feels, however remotely, that they have in some way been wronged, or that they weren't wholly to blame for their sin. But if that were actually true, then divine justice (as represented on the sign over the gates of Hell in Canto III) would be a farce, and God would be a capricious tyrant. It has taken some time for Dante to start to learn his lesson. Though he continues to feel pity at various places further down, here he starts to see sin for what it is: a filthy and dehumanizing rejection of God and His world. That kind of rejection, that kind of distortion of nature is not pitiable in the least. Which is why Virgil is so excited at what Dante says to Argenti, and why he says his desire to see Argenti further punished must be satisfied.

After Argenti is dealt with, the pilgrim hears the audible grief arising out of the city on the horizon, the great city of Dis. Drawing on the Saracen imagery from the crusades, Dante calls the towers "mosques" and sees them rising up in the distance, signifying the city of infidels. The walls and towers are covered with the host of fallen angels, who in anger (note its continued presence, linking the fifth circle with what will come after) keep the gates shut, refusing to let the travelers pass through. This is frustrating to Virgil, who up until this moment has been able to overcome the various guards, including, most recently, Phlegyas. But here, the demons present him with an obstacle he is not equipped to deal with. And this makes him angry (again, note the dominant emotion). His anger notwithstanding, he recognizes and comforts the pilgrim with the reality of the demons' ultimate impotence in the face of Heaven, and we are left awaiting help from above.

CANTO VIII: THE GATES OF DIS

Discussion Questions

1. Why does Dante backtrack his narrative to talk about his experience on the Styx?

2. What is the nature of wrath, and what might the surrounding muck signify?

3. Is the pilgrim's desire to see Argenti further punished righteous or unrighteous? Defend your answer.

4. What is the relationship between wrath and Argenti's self-devouring?

5. Speculate as to why Dante the poet might have ended the canto like he did, with the demons refusing the travelers passage.

CANTO IX

THE GATES OF DIS

Characters

- Dante and Virgil
- The Furies
- The Angel

Location

- Outside the city gates of Dis
- The Sixth Circle of Hell, the Circle of the Heresiarchs

Summary

After being rebuffed by the demons at the gates of Dis, Virgil returns to a stricken Dante, who pales at the realization that his guide has failed. Virgil tries to encourage him, but to no avail. He tells the pilgrim that he has been here before, all the way to the lowest circle of Hell, on an errand for the witch Erictho. As Virgil recounts his story, Dante is distracted by activity up on the top of the wall. The furies have arrived and summon Medusa, threatening to avenge themselves on Dante by turning him to stone. At that moment, however, help arrives. An angel from Heaven strides to the gates, preceded by a violent shaking of Hell. He opens the door without effort and severely chides the demons and the furies for their continued rebellion, reminding them of its supreme fruitlessness. The angel turns and leaves, allowing Virgil and Dante to enter without further resistance. The pilgrim discovers a wide plain, spotted all over with open graves out of which come horrible shrieks. These are the arch-heretics, formulators of doctrinal heresy, and their followers. Some tombs burn hotter than others, depending on how far from truth the teachings of their inhabitants were. The canto ends as they walk amongst the graves.

Notes

❖ 23: *conjured by that cruel witchqueen, Erictho*

Erictho is a witch in Lucan's *Pharsalia* (VI.507–830). The story of Virgil being sent by her was likely made up by Dante, though it resembles the Sybil who took Aeneas through the underworld. See the *Aeneid* VI.562–565.

❖ 27–29: *for a soul in the circle of Judas…*

The circle of Judas (Juddeca) is the lowest part of Hell, where those who betray their lords and benefactors are punished.

❖ 29: *furthest from that Heaven that turns all things*

The heaven that turns all things is the Empyrean Heaven,

where God is and from where He sets in motion the whole universe.

❖ 44: *of the queen of eternal weeping*

The "queen of eternal weeping" is Proserpina, the wife of Pluto. See the *Aeneid* IV.609–610 for her connection with the Furies.

❖ 45: *"Behold there, the ferocious Erinyes!"*

The Erinyes, or the Furies, were goddesses who inflicted punishment on criminals and the vicious. In some traditions the three sisters were born out of the blood that was produced when Cronus castrated his father Uranus. See Ovid's *Metamorphoses* IV.451–496, and Statius' *Thebaid* I.103–116.

❖ 52: *"Let come Medusa, and turn him to stone"*

Medusa was the youngest of the Gorgon sisters, and of the three was the only mortal. Her hair turned to snakes (like her older sisters) after she was violated by Neptune. She was beheaded by Perseus, though her head maintained its power of turning into stone whose who saw it. See Ovid's *Metamorphoses* IV.794–803.

❖ 54: *the war of Theseus was poorly made*

After Proserpina was abducted by Pluto, Theseus, the Athenian prince who slew the Minotaur, attempted a rescue mission (the "transgressive assault"), but failed. He was held captive until Hercules came and set him free. This is a slightly different version of the story represented in the *Aeneid* (VI.617–618) where Virgil has Theseus imprisoned for eternity.

⁜ 99: *still exhibits a skinned chin and gullet*

Cerberus received a "skinned chin and gullet" by being forcefully led up into the world on a chain by Hercules. See the *Aeneid* VI.391–397.

⁜ 112–114: *Such as at Arles, where the Rhone stagnates...*

Arles and Pola are both sites where Roman ruins and graveyards dominate the landscape.

⁜ 133: *we passed between the martyrs and high walls*

The Italian word *martíri* can be translated as either *martyrs* or *torments*. This translation has elected to use *martyrs* (both here and in line 2 of the following canto) for reasons that are explained more fully in the Analysis of *Paradiso* XV in the *Paradiso: Reader's Guide*.

Analysis

Walking through the gates of Dis represents entering into Hell proper. Upper Hell holds those who are punished for sins resulting from an inability to govern their own passions. As such, the souls we have encountered thus far have committed sins that are considered less serious. Their actions are more bestial than human, and so are in a sense less offensive. Lower Hell, starting with the heresiarchs that we will meet in the following canto, is the home of sinners who sinned in increasing measure against the intellect. This means they have sinned against the faculty that distinguishes man from beast, the faculty that identifies us as image bearers of

CANTO IX: THE GATES OF DIS

God. In this way the sins of the intellect are more offensive to God than the sins of the flesh. If sin is a mis-ordering of love, excessive love of inherently good things is less offensive than either a privation of love toward the right thing (the circles of the violent), or a misdirected love toward the wrong thing (the circles of the fraudulent). The violent (starting with the wrathful in Cantos VII–VIII) represent a transition between Upper and Lower Hell, where the passion of anger is mixed with an increasingly greater use of the intellect. The violence progresses from mere short-temperedness to violence against God, which is necessarily an intellectual violence.

This transition is represented in the scene that unfolds here at the gates of Dis. The Furies represent anger and violence in its purest form. They are spite personified, full of hate, eager to destroy the pilgrim by turning him to stone by means of the head of the Gorgon. It is a fitting reminder here, at the entrance to these lower circles, that no matter how intense the punishments get, or the wickedness of the sins represented, their apparent strength and intensity is only a hollow shell compared to the permanence and pure force of Heaven, as represented in the Angel. Dante and Virgil will encounter more obstacles, the further down they go. But they are obstacles only to those still encumbered with sin. To the one who has been glorified in holiness by the light of the beatific vision, even the fierce intensity and intimidation of the Furies is but dust and straw, less threatening than a fly, and less trouble than the greasy air. What this canto presents us with is the infinite contrast between the power of sin and the power of holiness. The former crumbles in on itself until it is nothing but impotent ash. The latter remains and intensifies in strength and glory. Something to ponder as the journey continues.

INFERNO READER'S GUIDE

Discussion Questions

1. Why did Dante the poet give Virgil this moment of failure? What does this suggest about the limits of the classical figure's competence?

2. Discuss the use of the Furies and Medusa. Is Dante simply throwing in mythological characters for fun? What purpose might they serve?

3. Dante the poet encourages us to "wonder at the teaching that hides itself / beneath the thick veil of these strange verses" (lines 61–63). Go ahead, wonder. Why might he address the reader this way? What is he asking you to consider?

4. The Angel arrives, according to the simile, like a violent wildfire. Compare/contrast the 'fire' of the angel with the fires of Hell.

5. With high disdain, the angel excoriates the demons for their vain attempts to frustrate the will of God. We might nod our heads in agreement, and so we should. But what might the angel say to us, in our less than heavenly moments? How can we understand this passage in light of our own personal understanding of sin and holiness?

CANTO X

HERESIARCHS

Characters

- Dante and Virgil
- Farinata
- Cavalcante de Cavalcanti

Location

- The Sixth Circle of Hell, the Circle of the Heresiarchs

Summary

Having entered the gates of Dis at the end of the previous canto, our pilgrim and his guide are walking among the open tombs of the heresiarchs, those chieftains of heresy and division within the church, as well as their followers. In this sense they are ironically identified as *martìri*, or martyrs, (it is a pun, as the Italian word also means 'torments'). But these are men who died as witnesses not of the true faith, but of their false distortions. Epicurus, who believed that the soul died with the body, is buried in the tomb next to the travelers. Frederick II and a certain Cardinal (probably one Cardinal Ottaviano degli Ubaldini) are also mentioned as being buried there, both of whom were Epicurean materialists. Dante asks Virgil if he will be able to talk to any of the souls here, seeing that the tombs are open. No sooner does he ask the question than he hears a voice ask him to stay and converse with him. It is Farinata, a Ghibelline from the previous generation. They discuss the conflict between the Ghibellines (the party of Farinata) and the Guelphs (the party of Dante). In the middle of their conversation, another soul appears. It is Cavalcante de' Cavalcanti, the father of Dante's long time friend and fellow poet, Guido Cavalcanti. Cavalcante looks for his son, and not seeing him, asks Dante where he is. Dante is confused, stumbles over his words, and implies (mistakenly) that Guido is dead. This is too much for Cavalcante, who falls back into the tomb. Farinata picks up where he left off. He obliquely refers to Dante's exile happening within the next four to five years. This makes the pilgrim worried. Virgil encourages him, and tells him to wait until he is with Beatrice, who will be able to answer his questions.

Notes

❖ 11: *when, from the Valley of Jehoshaphat*
For the Valley of Jehoshaphat, see Joel 3:2–3:

> I will gather all the nations,
> and bring them down

into the Valley of Jehoshaphat,
and will plead with them there for my people
and for my heritage Israel,
whom they have scattered among the nations,
and parted my land.
And they have cast lots for my people
and have given a boy for an harlot,
and sold a girl for wine, that they might drink."

❖ 14: *with Epicurus and his followers*

Epicurus (342–270 BC) and his followers taught that, because there was no afterlife, the absence of pain was the supreme good. In reaction to this teaching, Dante, in the *Convivio*, said the following:

> I say that of all stupidities that is the most foolish, the basest, and the most pernicious, which believes that after this life there is no other; for if we turn over all the scriptures both of the philosophers and of the other sage writers, all agree in this that within us there is a certain part that endures.[9]

❖ 32: *See there Farinata, standing erect*

The nineteenth-century Dante scholar Paget Toynbee offers the following biography of Farinata:

> Manente, called Farinata, son of Jacopo degli Uberti, the 'Saviour of Florence,' was born in Florence at the beginning of Cent. xiii; while still in his boyhood he witnessed the introduction into the city of the Guelf and Ghibel-

---

9 Dante, *Convivio*, 97–98.

line factions, of the latter of which his family became the leaders; in 1239 he became the head of his house, and in 1248 he took a prominent part in the expulsion of the Guelfs, who however returned in 1251, and a few years later (in 1258) expelled the Ghibellines in their turn, Farinata among them; the latter, who was now the acknowledged head of his party, took refuge with the rest of the Ghibelline exiles in Siena, 'come luogo sicuro e nido de' Ghibellini,' where he actively engaged in organizing the measures which led to the crushing defeat of the Florentine Guelfs and their allies at Montaperti, and left the Ghibellines masters of Tuscany (Sep. 4, 1260). After their victory the Ghibellines held a council at Empoli, about twenty miles from Florence, at which it was proposed by the deputies from Siena and Pisa that in order effectually to secure the ascendency of their party, and to put an end once for all to the power of the Florentines, the city of Florence should be razed to the ground. Tothisproposal,which was approved by the majority of the assembly, Farinata offered the most determined opposition, declaring that he would defend his native city with his own sword as long as he had breath in his body, even though he should have to do it single-handed. In consequence of this vehement protest the proposal was abandoned and Florence was saved from destruction. The Florentines, however, subsequently showed little gratitude to their fellow-citizen for his patriotic intervention, for they always expressly included the Uberti with the other Ghibelline families who were excepted from the terms offered to the other exiles. After Montaperti Farinata returned to Florence, where he died in or about 1264, the year before Dante's birth. A few years later, at a time when an attempt was made to reconcile the Guelf and Ghibelline factions in Florence by means of matrimonial alliances, a daughter of Farinata was betrothed to the Guelf Guido Cavalcanti, and the marriage was subsequently carried into effect.[10]

❖ 52: *At that very moment a shade arose*

Cavalcante de' Cavalcanti, father of Dante's friend Guido, was a Guelph and an Epicurean. Furthermore, he was the father-in-law of Farinata's daughter.

❖ 60: *where is my son? Why is he not with you?*

Guido Cavalcanti, a White Guelph, was violently opposed to the Black Guelphs (the faction that would later exile Dante from Florence). In 1300, the hostilities between the two factions had grown to such a fever pitch that the prior of Florence, one of which was Dante, exiled the prominent leaders of both the Blacks and the Whites, one of which was Guido. Thus, for the sake of peace in Florence, Dante was forced to exile his own friend. Even though the exiles were soon recalled, Guido never returned for shortly after he left Florence, he contracted malaria and died.

❖ 79–81: *But not fifty times will the face of her...*

Dante's exile happening within the next four to five years is determined by the reference to "the face of her / who reigns here below" in Hell, or Proserpina, who was also the goddess of the Moon. Hence, her face being rekindled fifty times refers to fifty full moons, or, fifty months.

---

10 Paget Toynbee, *Dante Dictionary* (Oxford: Clarendon Press, 1898), 227.

∵ 85–87: *Wherefore I answered, "The great massacre…"*

"The great massacre" that "dyed the Arbia red" refers to the decisive Ghibelline victory at Montaperti in 1260. This is a battle that will be referenced again.

∵ 119–120: *here within is the second Frederick…*

Frederick II, the Holy Roman Emperor from 1215–1250, and Cardinal Ottaviano (d. 1273) both disbelieved in the permanence of the soul after death.

Analysis

"All will one day be bolted shut, / when, from the Valley of Jehoshaphat, / they return with their bodies that perished" (lines 10–12). Thus Virgil explains to the pilgrim, referring first to the shutting of these open tombs here inside the gates of Dis, but also, more generally, to the finality of the second death. On that day, Virgil is saying, all the souls in these tombs will rise again from the dead, in the great resurrection (see Joel 3, John 5:29), be reunited with their flesh, and then be sent back to their places in this sixth circle, and there be sealed forever in their grave. Thus everyone, blessed and damned, will receive their body again, and in that enfleshed state, either enjoy or suffer eternity. While a hard doctrine, it is one that has ample support in Scripture, and is not seriously contested. Furthermore, it leads into the two points Dante is making. First, he has this doctrine vocalized by Virgil. This is fascinating, because the Roman poet represents complete natural knowledge, without the special revelation of Scripture. Thus Dante is making the point that even without Scripture, it is possible (and, perhaps, even necessary) to infer from this natural world, two things: 1) our souls are indestructible, and 2) our souls are ultimately incomplete without the body; two things which infer the eternality of the body. The second point of interest is that the very next lines following the ones quoted above, tell us that they are standing in front of the grave of Epicurus, who taught that the soul died with the body. This is basic materialism. Materialism teaches that there is no life after death, the soul is not immortal, and the material world is the whole show. Notice the rich irony in what Virgil says in front of the Epicureans. Not only do these Epicureans now realize they were wrong, that the soul is in fact immortal, that it continues past death; but what is more, on that final day they will actually regain the flesh as well, to which they gave ultimacy. And in that body/soul unity, they will be eternally sealed in the tomb of their heretical beliefs.

Discussion Questions

1. Discuss the implications of the punishment these souls suffer: being buried in Hell. What is the significance of burial, especially for Epicureans?

2. Why are there, relatively speaking, so many surprises in this canto? Farinata startles Dante, Cavelcante interrupts Farinata, Cavelcante is surprised at hearing (mistakenly) that his son is dead, Dante is disturbed by Farinata's prediction, etc.

3. Dante is unafraid (as we have seen already) of putting anyone in Hell. In this canto alone, we have a king, a clergyman, a military figure, and a philosopher. But is Dante populating Hell simply with those that he dislikes? Or is there something deeper going on? (Hint: there is.)

4. What do you make of Farinata's explanation that the souls in Hell are given enough light from God to see things that are far off in the future, though of human activity that is near or present, they have no knowledge? Is this just a plot device?

5. Discuss the possible reasons for Cavelcante randomly interrupting Farinata and asking about his son.

CANTO XI

DISCOURSE ON THE STRUCTURE OF HELL

Characters

❖ Dante and Virgil

Location

❖ The border between the Sixth and Seventh Circles

Summary

The stench rising up from Lower Hell is so strong that Virgil decides to wait awhile until their senses grow accustomed to it. As they wait, Dante asks his guide to fill the time with some beneficial discourse. Virgil obliges and describes the structure of Hell. It becomes clear that Dante the poet wishes us to think of Hell as a giant funnel, with circles growing smaller the further down one goes. Lower Hell, circles seven through nine, are populated by the violent and the fraudulent. The seventh circle is divided into three sections, or wheels, in which are punished those violent against neighbor, against self, and against God, respectively. In the eighth circle are punished those who committed fraud against strangers. In the ninth circle, the lowest point of Hell, Earth, and all the universe, where Dis (or Satan) himself is imprisoned, are punished those who committed fraud against friends. Dante, appreciative of this explanation, asks why these are divided from those who are punished outside of the gates of Dis. Virgil reminds him that, according to Aristotle, vice can be divided into three categories: incontinence, malice, and bestiality (malice and bestiality representing fraud and violence respectively). But because sins of incontinence are the least rational of the vices, they are less offensive to God, and so are punished in Upper Hell. Following this, Dante seeks clarification on a certain point about usurers and how they offend against the bounty of God. Virgil, referencing Aristotle again, notes that art (or human industry) follows nature (divine industry). Thus an appreciation and respect for nature and her student, human industry, are necessary for human flourishing. The usurer disparages both, "placing [his] hope elsewhere." Though this is oblique, Virgil is probably saying that, instead of trusting to God's goodness in creation and man's duty to work hard, the usurer trusts only in himself to the point of doing violence to "the divine bounty." Noting the position of the constellations (were they visible), Virgil decides the time has come to go. It is around 4am on the morning of Holy Saturday.

CANTO XI: DISCOURSE ON THE STRUCTURE OF HELL

Notes

∴ 8: *that stated, "I guard Pope Anastasius"*

"Pope Anastasius" is likely a mixture of a pope and an emperor, both from the late fifth century, both named Anastatius. It was probably the emperor Anastatius, and not the pope of that name, that was led away by Photinus into a certain form of Arianism, denying the full divinity of Jesus.

∴ 16–90: *"My son," he began, "within these rent rocks…"*

Dante's whole systematizing of Hell in terms of Incontinence, Violence, and Fraud, laid out in this canto is founded on a doctrine of vice from Aristotle (his *Ethics*), and developed by Aquinas (his *Summa*), but with Dante's own special flair thrown in for good measure.

∴ 50: *on both Sodom and Cahors and he who*

"Sodom and Cahors" refer to the sins of homosexuality and usury, respectively; both of which are punished in the third wheel of the seventh circle.

∴ 80: *with which your* Ethics *touches on the three*

See Aristotle's *Nicomachean Ethics* VII, 1.1145a.

∴ 81: *dispositions that Heaven does not will?*

For Dante's use of the word *dispositions* (*disposizion*) and its identification with habit, see Aquinas' *Summa Theologiae* I–II, q. 49, a. 2, ad 3, and Aristotle's *Metaphysics* V, 20, 1022b.

❖ 83–84: *That incontinence...*

For this doctrine of "less reproach" see the *Summa Theologiae* I–II, q. 78, a. 4, resp. where Aquinas says,

> A sin committed through malice is more grievous than a sin committed through passion, for three reasons. First, because, as sin consists chiefly in an act of the will, it follows that, other things being equal, a sin is all the more grievous, according as the movement of the sin belongs more to the will. Now when a sin is committed through malice, the movement of sin belongs more to the will, which is then moved to evil of its own accord, than when a sin is committed through passion, when the will is impelled to sin by something extrinsic, as it were. Wherefore a sin is aggravated by the very fact that it is committed through certain malice, and so much the more, as the malice is greater; whereas it is diminished by being committed through passion, and so much the more, as the passion is stronger.[11]

❖ 101: *and also, if you note your* Physics *well*

See Aristotle's *Physics* II.2.194a and II.8.198a.

❖ 113–114: *the Fish dart up across the horizon...*

The constellation Pisces, or the Fish, has risen above the horizon in the northern hemisphere; the Great Bear, what we call the Big Dipper, is above Corus's winds, that is, in the northwest. In other words, it is around 4am.

---

[11] https://www.newadvent.org/summa/2078.htm#article4

CANTO XI: DISCOURSE ON THE STRUCTURE OF HELL

Analysis

It is unusual for modern Christians to rank sins in terms of offensiveness to God. All sin is sin, we say. Scripture is clear, if you have broken one part of the law, you have broken the whole of it (James 2:10). Sometimes, in comparing white lies to genocide, we recognize that certain sins can be far more destructive than others; but at the same time we know that all sin, no matter its level of destructiveness, separates us from God, and that God hates all of it. So it can be a little unnerving to read someone say that a certain kind of sin displeases God less than another, as if He is not equally displeased with all sin, and every manner of sin. But if we try and understand what Dante is doing here, I think we will find a helpful paradigm for understanding not just the nature of sin, but the nature of man as well.

It is important to note that there are no references to the Ten Commandments in Dante's Hell. And the reason is they are a part of special revelation. But for divine justice to be upheld in Hell, according to Dante and medieval thought, the damned must be held to a standard they would have known in their life, and would have been able to agree with. Therefore, without the Ten Commandments a different standard (or rather, a different expression of the same standard, which is God's immutable nature) must exist as the standard of virtuous living. Dante creates his Hell along the lines of what man, in his natural state, with the law of God written on his heart can know about good and evil (see Romans 2:12–16). This is why Aristotle is held up as the authority. Natural law (as distinguished from God's Moral Law, though the one is an outflow of the other) is objective and recognized across cultures and centuries.

We've touched on this already a number of times, but Canto XI is where Dante brings it all together. The three categories of sins mentioned here are species consistently experienced by man. Incontinence is allowing passions and appetites to overrule reason; violence is the forceful manipulation of others for the sake of one's own ends; fraud is the intellectual manipulation of others for the sake of one's own gain. The primary element that distinguishes the three categories is the level to which one's will and intellect are in use. The rational capacity of man is the very thing that distinguishes him from the animal world, and therefore the most important aspect that likens him to God. Thus, the more the intellect is involved in the sin, the more of an affront it is to the image of God. It is in this sense that incontinence is less displeasing to God, and fraud earns the heaviest sentence. Violence holds a position between the two, as it is equal parts willful action and emotional outburst.

Even though we know everyone is equally damned, equally in Hell, this system allows Dante to pass along the helpful insights belonging to Natural law. It elucidates the nature of man, and the various natures of man's specific modes of rebellion against God. To distinguish between lust and fraud is not to minimize the hatefulness of the one in the face of the other. Rather it is to identify the difference between an excessive love for something inherently good (incontinence, or lack of self-restraint), a deficient love for something good (violence, or brutishness), and a love oriented around the wrong object (fraud, or vicious malice). Reading Dante this way (as this canto especially makes clear) reminds us that he is not first and foremost interested in giving an exact and detailed account of the afterlife. Rather he is more interested in the soul's journey toward God, which is man's chief end. And the first step in that journey is understanding the different ways we can be distracted from that end. This becomes all the more important as the various habits these particular sins are manifestations of get corrected in *Purgatorio*, as man is sanctified by the grace of the Holy Spirit.

Discussion Questions

1. Is there a reason Dante includes the tombstone of Pope Anastasius at the beginning of this canto? What relevance does he have to the subsequent conversation?

2. Based on Virgil's discourse here, how would you define injustice? Justice?

3. Explain the three kinds of Violence. Explain the two kinds of Fraud.

4. Violence against self is most clearly evidenced in suicide. But Dante also claims that weeping one ought to be light-hearted and glad is also a form of violence, in particular, violence against one's own things. Do you agree with this assessment? What might Dante be getting at here?

5. Explain the difference between those punished inside the city of Dis, and those punished outside and above. Are these distinctions helpful? If so, how?

6. In the discussion of the usurer, Virgil brings up the difference between nature and human industry (art). What is going on here, and in what way does the usurer disparage both?

CANTO XII

TYRANTS AND ROBBERS

Characters

❖ Dante and Virgil

❖ The Centaurs: Nessus, Chiron, and Pholus

❖ Alexander the Great (or Alexander of Pherae), Dinoysus, of Syracuse, Azzolino da Romano, Obizzo de Este, Guy de Monfort ("a shade apart"), Atilla the Hun, Pyrrhus, Sextus Pompey, and Rinier da Cornato and Rinier Pazzo (famous Florentine highwaymen)

Location

❖ The Seventh Circle, the First Wheel: the Tyrants and Robbers, Violence against Neighbor and their Goods

Summary

Having finished his discourse, Virgil is ready to leave the sixth circle and scramble down the cliff to the seventh.

But at the edge of the cliff they are blocked by the Minotaur, the mythical beast of Crete. The Roman poet taunts the creature, momentarily paralyzing it with anger. With the Minotaur distracted, Virgil and Dante are able to get by. Once they make it down the cliff face, broken and fragmented by the Harrowing of Hell, they meet a vast company of centaurs. Virgil asks them for a guide to show them how to proceed, a request that they grant. At the chief centaur Chiron's command, Nessus leads them along a circular trench filled with boiling blood, which is the place reserved for those who were violent against their neighbor. However, as Virgil noted in the previous canto, violence can be directed against either the person or that which belongs to the person (a distinction that continues in the next two wheels). Thus, submerged within the boiling stream are both tyrants, those violent against the person, and robbers, those violent against that person's goods. The varying degrees of their sin's effects determine how deep the souls are plunged beneath the blood, from fully covered to blood lapping the feet. If the souls try to raise themselves higher than they ought, the centaurs are ready with bows and arrows to shoot them back down. Nessus points out several souls and alludes to their crimes: Alexander the Great, Dionysus of Syracuse, Azzolino da Romano, Obizzo da Este, Guy de Montfort ("a shade set apart"), Atilla the Hun, Pyrrhus, Sextus Pompey, Rinier da Corneto and Rinier Pazzo (two famous Florentine highwaymen). When they come to the part of the stream that is most shallow, they cross over and the centaur returns to his troop.

CANTO XII: TYRANTS AND ROBBERS

Notes

⁂ *12–27: the infamy of Crete stretched itself out…*

The story of how Pasiphae, wife of Minos, when he was the king of Crete, fell in love with a bull, and had Daedalus build her a hollow wooden cow ("counterfeit"), into which she climbed and received the amorous advances of the bull, thus conceiving and giving birth to the Minotaur, is told in Ovid's *Metamorphoses* VIII.131–137, and in other places as well. Theseus, the Duke of Athens, eventually killed the Minotaur by the help of its half-sister, Ariadne.

⁂ *32–45: "You are perhaps thinking of this ruin…"*

The *ruin blocked by this bestial wrath* was the result of Christ descending into Sheol (Limbo) to rescue the faithful who were waiting for Him. In doing so, He shook Hell to pieces, and from here on out we will see signs of that destructive force. However, that had not yet happened when Virgil made his previous journey.

⁂ *67–69: He nudged me, and said, "That one is Nessus…"*

Nessus was in love with Hercules' wife Deianira. When he attempted to rape her, Hercules killed him with a poisoned arrow. In revenge, before he died, Nessus gave Deianira his own cloak, soaked in his poisoned blood, to give to Hercules. Not knowing the cloak was infected, she did. Putting it on, Hercules was driven crazy, and eventually killed himself. Thus Nessus "made for himself his own revenge." See Ovid's *Metamorphoses* IX.127–162.

∴ 65: *to Chiron there beside you; to your hurt*

Chiron, son of Saturn, was Achilles' tutor for a season, along with Jason and other classical figures. He was the wisest of all centaurs.

∴ 72: *Last is Pholus, who was so full of rage.*

Pholus was another acquaintance of Hercules, who either killed himself accidentally with one of Hercules' poisoned arrows, or was killed by Bacchus. See Ovid's *Metamorphoses* XIII.306 and Lucan's *Pharsalia* VI.391.

∴ 101: *beside the bank of boiling vermillion*

Notice the fourth instance of the adjective *vermillion*, this time describing the color of the boiling blood in the river.

∴ 107: *There is Alexander*

Alexander could also refer to Alexander of Pherae (a contemporary of Alexander the Great in the fourth century BC), who had a reputation for barbaric acts of violence. Dionysus of Syracuse lived during the same time as well. Azzolino, a Ghibelline, was son-in-law of the previously mentioned Frederick II, in the early part of the thirteenth century. Obizzo, a Guelph, died in 1293, at the hands of Azzo, his son-in-law. All these men were notoriously violent rulers. Guy de Monfort killed his cousin in a church ("within the womb of God") while mass was being given. His cousin's heart was placed in a casket on top of the London Bridge. Atilla the Hun made a nuisance of himself to both sides of the Roman Empire in the fifth century; Pyrrhus, king of Epirus, died in 275 BC; Sextus was the younger son of Pompey the Great, and was a pirate. As mentioned above, the two Riniers were famous

Florentine highwaymen. Among these we see both those violent against their neighbor, and those violent against their neighbor's goods.

Analysis

This canto is full of halves: the half-man, half-bull Minotaur; the half-man, half-horse centaurs; and the partly exposed men poking out of the boiling blood. This is significant in that the region of Hell populated by the violent exists between Upper Hell, where incontinent are punished, and Lower Hell, where the fraudulent are punished. The incontinent are subject to their passions and emotions, and do not govern themselves with reason. This lack of reason makes them functional beasts. The fraudulent are those that put their intellectual powers to wicked ends. Because reason is what distinguishes man from the beasts, a capacity that identifies man as the image of God, the perverted and wicked use of reason is a more heinous violation of justice. Violence occupies a middle place between these poles, not just in location, but in experience. Violence is both intellectual, in that it is premeditated and purposeful, and it is also passionate, in that the violent are overtaken by their anger to the point where their intellect takes a back seat (witness the Minotaur paralyzed by his rage). The Creten monster and the centaurs both represent this hideous admixture of passion and intellect, but in opposite ways. The Minotaur has a human body with the head of a bull, whereas the centaurs have the bodies of a horse with a human torso and head. The Minotaur is more passionately violent, where the centaurs are more violent in a rational way (they choose their arrows, and identify their targets with precision). Notice too, the difference between the souls punished here and the wrathful punished in the fifth circle. The souls submerged in the Styx in Canto VIII bite, gnaw, and chew one another. They are controlled not by reason, but by the passion of anger. Thus they are punished in Upper Hell, though at the lowest point of that region. They serve as the transition between the incontinent and the violent. Here, in the seventh circle, the sinners are more controlled, as they consciously suffer the boiling blood, reflecting the presence of the intellect and will in their sin.

Remembering Virgil's discourse on the sin of violence, one can be violent against others, against self, and against God. Additionally, violence can be directed both against the object and/or that which rightly belongs to the object. Here, in this first wheel of the 7th Circle, those who were violent against other men (tyrants like Alexander) and/or against their goods (thieves and robbers like the two Riniers) are punished. And they are punished by being boiled in blood. The boiling blood identifies the reason why they are not in Lower Hell, in that their hot-tempered passions got the better of them. Furthermore, blood stands both for human life and, more obliquely, for the substance of their life. And so for those who trafficked in both those "goods", it is fitting that their punishment should be a complete giving over to their sin. Divine justice, according to Romans 1:24 works this way, as hardened hearts are given over to themselves. Hell is the ultimate expression of that. Those who take the blood of others, and die in their sins, receive nothing but that blood eternally after.

Discussion Questions

1. Read Ephesians 4:8–9 and 1 Peter 3:18–22. Tie this into Dante's reference to the Harrowing of Hell, "that great plunder of souls."

2. Discuss the legitimacy of variegated punishments. How can it be useful for understanding the nature of sin?

3. What do the half-creatures represent? Why are they an important part of the narrative?

4. What is the relationship between violence and incontinence? Between violence and fraud? Why does it occupy a middle position?

5. I offered an explanation of boiling blood in the analysis. Do you agree or disagree? What do you think it might represent?

CANTO XIII

SUICIDES AND SQUANDERERS

Characters

∴ Dante and Virgil
∴ Pier della Vigna (minister for Frederick II)
∴ Lano da Siena and Jacopo da Santo Andrea
∴ An unknown Florentine suicide

Location

∴ The Seventh Circle, The Second Wheel: the Suicides and Squanderers, Violence against Self and One's Own Goods

Summary

As the centaur Nessus returns, Dante and Virgil make their way into the second wheel, which appears to be a dense wood. This is the circle of the suicides and squanderers, those violent against self and their own property. The pilgrim hears a tremendous howling all around him, although he sees no one. The only creatures he sees are the Harpies, nesting in the barren branches, continually nibbling at the twigs. In order for Dante to understand what is going on, Virgil tells him to break off the end of a branch of one of the trees. Doing so, Dante is taken aback as blood and steam bubble out of the end of the piece in his hand; and with the blood, a voice. Though not named, this is the soul of Pier della Vigna, who was the minister of Frederick II. His soul resides in the tree, and is made one with it, as punishment for his suicide. As his story makes clear, he was falsely accused out of envy, and disdaining the "disdain," he took his own life. Virgil questions him regarding what will happen to these souls in the final resurrection. The soul of Pier explains that they, like everyone else, will rise again to claim their bodies. However they will not be permitted to put them back on. Instead, they will each return to their own tree with their corpses hung on the branches of their prison. After he finishes this explanation, two frenzied souls not imprisoned in trees (Lano da Siena and Jacopo da Santo Andrea) rush past them, calling after one another. They are being chased by a pack of greyhound-like demons, who tear them apart with their teeth, and carry them back. They are two squanderers, and their punishment is to be chased and mauled. This event leads Dante and Virgil to a different tree, where the soul of an unnamed Florentine suicide speaks of his city. As Florence was Christianized, they repurposed a temple originally dedicated to Mars (their first patron) and rededicated it to John the Baptist. As a punishment for this betrayal, this unnamed soul suggests, Mars continues to make Florence sad "through his art"; in other words, through continual war and strife, Mars will have his revenge on Christianity. The canto ends as the travelers discover that the soul of this suicide took his life, having made for himself a gallows out of his house.

Notes

❖ 8: *between the Cecina and Corneto*

The river Cecina and the town of Corneto form the boundaries of the Maremma region in Tuscany that was well-known for its thick vegetation.

❖ 10–12: *There the barbaric Harpies make their nests...*

The Harpies were monstrous birds of prey with the face and sometimes body of a woman. For the hunting of the Trojans, see the *Aeneid* III.209–257.

❖ 48: *"that which he has only seen in my rhyme"*

Virgil is here referencing the following passage in the *Aeneid* III.22–48,

> I was sacrificing
> To Venus my mother and to the other gods
> That they might bless the work I had embarked on;
> And to the Monarch of all the Heaven-dwellers
> I was about to slay a glossy bull
> On the seashore. Now there chanced to be nearby
> A mound whose top was thick with a scrub of cornel
> And myrtle shoots as stiff and sharp as spears.
> I went there and I tried to uproot some greenery,
> To grace the altar with a leafy canopy,
> When I was met by an awesome and ghastly marvel:
> From the first tree I wrenched at, tearing it off
> At the roots, blood welled up in black drops
> And sullied the earth with its spots. A chill shudder
> Convulsed my body and my blood froze with fear.
> I tried again and tugged at the stubborn stems
> Of a second tree, to try and find out the cause

> Of the mystery. Another gout of blood
> Broke from the bark. In a moil of puzzled wonder
> I began to pray to the nymphs of the countryside
> And Father Mars, the god of Thrace; I besought them
> To turn the vision to good and to purge off
> The horror of the omen: but when I tried
> To uproot the third stem, straining with my knees
> Dug into the sand and my whole body braced
> For a greater effort—oh shall I dare to tell
> What happened, or keep silent?—from the depths
> Of the mound I heard heartrending moans and I heard
> A human voice: 'Aeneas,' it cried out, 'why
> Must you tear me apart, suffering as I am?
> Let me alone, at last, in my grave stain not
> Your innocent hands with guilt. I am no stranger;
> I am of Troy it is Trojan blood you see
> Weep from that branch. Fly from these cruel lands!
> Fly from these misers' shores! I am Polydorus.
> And here I lie where an iron crop of spears
> First laid me low, and out of my buried body
> Shoot stems as weapon-sharp.'
>   Then indeed I stood
> Dumfounded in a maze of doubt and dread
> My hair stood up, my voice stuck in my throat.[12]

✥ *115–138: And behold, two came up on our left side…*

Lano da Siena (member of the "Spendthrift Club"; see Canto XXIX) and Jacopo da Santo Andrea (of Padua) were both prodigals who wasted their respective fortunes wildly and recklessly.

---

12 Virgil, *Aeneid*, tr. Patric Dickinson, (New York: Mentor, 1961), 53–54.

CANTO XIII: SUICIDES AND SQUANDERERS

Analysis

With what is perhaps the most unusual punishment we have encountered so far, the souls of the suicides are forced into a union with infernal thorn bushes, instead of being given a shade that echoes their earthly bodies. This denial of the human form coincides with their rejection of the body that they held in contempt (the Italian word used is *molesta*, line 108). Indeed, it is the soul's rejection of the body, a photo negative of the Epicurean heresy of the body's rejection of the soul. Man was created to be both body and soul, an ensouled body and embodied soul. In that unity, he bears the image of God as God created him to exist. Physical death is the corruption, or separation of that unity, a physical symbol of the separation that death brings between man and God. To force that separation through suicide is an act of high rebellion against God, and against human nature. It is a rejection of the creational unity, and, indirectly, a violence not only against self, but against all people. In despising one's own body/soul unity, the suicide is rejecting and holding in contempt that which makes every person a person. At its root it is a misunderstanding of what man is. He is not a duality ("my unjust self against my just self," line 72). He does not have two selves. He is one self—body and soul together. Therefore, the suicide's punishment consists of never being able to assume that body again. Instead, they must take on the foreign "flesh" of a thorn bush (alluding to the thorns and thistles of the curse; see Genesis 3). Their unrepentant sin being an outworking of the curse, they must embrace the curse all the way and become their own plague. In this form they are eternally torn and gnawed by the Harpies.

The suicides inability to ever inhabit a body again brings up a biblical truth not often discussed today. In the final resurrection at the end of time, everybody will be raised again into an immortal body. It is in those immortal bodies that the saved are led into eternal life, and the damned are cast into eternal death, or (in the context of this poem) back into their respective circles in Hell. So it is that the suicides will rise to receive their bodies (their "remains") but instead of inhabiting them again, they will drag them back down to the second wheel of the seventh circle, and hang their corpses on the trees they will be forced to be united to again. This is interesting on many levels but of greatest importance here is the significance of the human body. Throughout the *Comedy* (especially in *Paradiso*) Dante makes reference to the chief hope of the saints being a reunification with their bodies. This is not because of some misplaced pride in, or love for, their own selves, but rather a recognition that with the resurrection comes the restoration of how they were created to be. Death is terrible; even for those in Paradise, where there is no suffering, it represents for the shades an incompleteness to their joy. Death is the corruption of what God made whole. Which again, is why suicide, in Dante's understanding, is such a violent rejection both of God and of His nature.

A quick note on the other characters in this wheel: the squanderers. The two shades running from the hell hounds were notorious prodigals in their day. Dante conceives of this kind of sin differently than those souls in the fourth circle. The spendthrifts there were punished for their incontinence, their inability to allow reason to govern their spending. Here, given the circle they are in, and the nature of this middle region, there is something of the intellect mixed in with their passion for sinful largesse. In this way Dante classifies the

CANTO XIII: SUICIDES AND SQUANDERERS

squanderers as violent not against self, but against one's own goods. This is sinful because just as the body is given to people for a purpose, for wisdom and virtue and worship, so too are the goods they receive given for that same purpose. To squander it willfully and purposefully, is to do violence against those goods, and thus against God's gift. The squanderers are punished gruesomely by being ripped apart, a testimony to how prodigality, in reality, though unlike the suicides, truly is a ripping apart of one's own self.

Discussion Questions

1. What do the Harpies add to this canto? Why are they important?

2. Why does Dante (through the soul of Pier) liken envy to a whore?

3. Why does Pier say that the Harpies both "cause pain" and also make "for the pain an outlet"?

4. Discuss the inverse relationship between suicides and the Epicureans.

5. What is the relationship between the squanderers and their punishment? Of what significance are the hell hounds? Is there any resemblance to the she-wolf of Canto I and what she represents?

6. Why do you think the unnamed suicide spends so much time talking about Florence? What is going on there?

CANTO XIV

BLASPHEMERS, SODOMITES, AND USURERS

Characters

❖ Dante and Virgil

❖ Capaneus

Location

❖ The Seventh Circle, The Third Wheel: the Blasphemers, Sodomites, and Usurers, Violence against God and His own Goods (or Nature)

Summary

After our pilgrim gathers the fallen leaves beneath the shrub of the unknown Florentine, he and his guide move on to the third wheel of the seventh circle, a broad wasteland of burning sand. Flakes of flame continuously fall down on the three sets of sinners punished in this wheel: the blasphemers, those violent against God directly; the sodomites, those violent against nature (God's property); and the usurers, those violent against nature's goods. The first group contains the fewest number of sinners, but their groanings and shrieks are the loudest. The second group is the most populated, and they walk continuously around the burning plain. The third group we will not meet until Canto XVII. This canto deals only with one blasphemer, Capaneus. He is famous for being one of the seven kings who fought against Thebes. A giant of a man, with an ego to match, he arrogantly railed against Zeus, claiming that even the god could not stop him from destroying Thebes. His blasphemy against Zeus (or Jove, as Dante referred to him) was counted as an offense against the true God, and so is punished here. Like the other blasphemers, he must lie on his back, facing up (the direction of the heavens), and suffer under the continual rain of fire. This posture emphasizes his helplessness and impotence to actually fight against God. After a brief interaction with this soul, Virgil enters into a further description of the topography of Hell, explaining the source of the four rivers, or stagnate pools ("stagni"), by means of the mythological/allegorical statue on the island of Crete. Dante was expecting to see Lethe as well, the other river of the underworld in ancient mythology; but Virgil tells him he will only see it once he leaves this pit, intimating that they will come to it at the top of Mount Purgatory. With these questions discussed, they make their way across the sands.

CANTO XIV: BLASPHEMERS, SODOMITES, AND USURERS

Notes

❖ 15: *once trod under by the feet of Cato*

Cato's march over the sands of Libya are detailed in Lucan's *Pharsalia* IX.371–410.

❖ 31–36: *Like Alexander, in those hot regions…*

The story of Alexander the Great ordering his troops to trample the falling fire-flakes is probably from a work of Thomas Aquinas' teacher, Albertus Magnus, *De meteoris* I, iv, 8.

❖ 56: *in shifts at Mongibello, calling out*

Mongibello was another name for Mount Etna where the blacksmith god, Vulcan, kept his workshops. For the story of Vulcan and the Cyclopes ("the others" in line 55) forging the thunderbolts of Zeus, see the *Aeneid* VIII.416–422.

❖ 63–72: *"O Capaneus, unextinguished pride…"*

The figure and story of Capaneus is taken from Statius's *Thebaid* X.883–939.

❖ 69: *who besieged Thebes; he held God in contemp*

The *Thebaid* of Statius tells the story of this famous siege of Thebes.

❖ 79: *As the brook flows from the Bulicame*

Bulicame refers to a site where there were natural hot springs, around which prostitutes would set up their houses.

∵ 100: *Rhea chose it as a trusted cradle*

Rhea was the wife of Cronus and mother of many gods and goddesses, including Zeus. Zeus is the son here referenced. See Obid's *Fasti* IV.197–214.

∵ 104: *who keeps his back turned from Damietta*

Damietta is down along the Nile, in Egypt.

Analysis

On the island of Crete (per Virgil's explanation), there is a cave in which stands a large statue of an old man (representing mankind), facing Rome, with his back to the East. A head of gold (representing the golden, prelapsarian age) sits on a chest of silver, with a belly of brass, legs and a left foot of iron, and a terra-cotta right foot. This image combines both Nebuchadnezzar's statue from Daniel 2, and the ancient metallic classification of the ages. What is more, according to all the earliest commentaries, the two feet represent the twin authorities of the church and the empire, a common theme in Dante. The right foot (the church) is more frail but also the more foundational, as the statue stands more erect on that foot than on the other. The whole body, save the head, is cracked (representing the Fall) and through this crack tears continually pour out. Those tears (representing the pain of the curse) cascade down into the deep infernal valley, and feed the four pools: Acheron, Styx, Phlegethon, and Cocytus. Dante remembers crossing the first two, and knows that the fourth one is coming; however he is confused about the third. Virgil tells him it is the stream

CANTO XIV: BLASPHEMERS, SODOMITES, AND USURERS

of boiling blood they have just recently crossed in the first wheel of the seventh circle (in Canto XII).

Coming back to the two different feet, in the concluding sentences of *De Monarchia*, as we saw in the Introduction, Dante says, "Let Caesar therefore show that reverence towards Peter which a firstborn son should show his father, so that, illumined by the light of paternal grace, he may the more effectively light up the world, over which he has been placed by Him alone who is ruler over all things spiritual and temporal." Dante held that God had ordained the Roman Empire (and then the Holy Roman Empire) to govern the world, and that empire was the greatest form of civil government. This was distinct, of course, from the spiritual authority on earth which was the Church, figured in the Pope. Thus the state is pictured as the "firstborn son" of Father Church. If all worked as it ought to, the Church would govern the spiritual lives of men, and the empire would watch over their external needs; further the empire would do so in a manner congruent with and obedient to the teachings and exhortations of the Church.

Anyone familiar with the works of Abraham Kuyper might recognize here an early version of sphere sovereignty. God has ordained different spheres of government in the world, with different authority figures in each sphere: the state with authority over civil matters, the Church over spiritual ones. Dante was a major proponent of this separation of authority, with both the Church and the empire existing directly beneath, and indeed both commissioned by, the ultimate rule of Christ. It was his greatest wish that both the Holy Roman Emperor and the Pope would be duly recognized in their respective positions, and even more so because they were governing well. It is because neither hardly ever did that so many rulers and so many popes populate the ditches of Hell.

Discussion Questions

1. Dante takes Capaneus' blasphemy against Jove and calls that defiance against God. How does he do this? What are the implications of this kind of move?

2. Discuss the punishment of the proud, in their supine position. Why is that a potent image?

3. What is the meaning behind the barren and burning sand and the eternally falling flame-flakes? What might it have to do with the nature of violence against God/nature?

4. Discuss the various aspects of the statue in the cave, especially the fact that the frail terra-cotta foot is more foundational than the strong iron foot.

5. What is the poetic impact of Dante's using mythological artifacts to construct his underworld?

CANTO XV

BLASPHEMERS, SODOMITES, AND USURERS

Characters

❖ Dante and Virgil

❖ Brunetto Latino

❖ Priscian, Francesco d'Accorso, and Andrea de' Mozzi (the "scruff")

Location

❖ The Seventh Circle, The Third Wheel: the Blasphemers, Sodomites, and Usurers; Violence against God and His own Goods (or Nature)

Summary

Having left the blasphemers lying prone on the ground, our pilgrim now encounters the sodomites, who continuously walk around. As they come to a particular group, one of the damned cries out, recognizing Dante. It is Brunetto Latino (also known as Latini), who was a significant figure in Dante's own development, though more of an influence than an actual teacher. A tender and intimate scene unfolds as the two come together, albeit with a touch of melancholy as this meeting is, after all, happening in Hell. Latino, with the foresight given to the damned, warns of the coming turmoil in Dante's life. Dante affirms that he is ready for Fortune's wheel, come what may. Further, he assures Brunetto that he will confer with Beatrice (the "wise lady", literally "a lady who will know"). Following this, their conversation turns to others there who are of note. This first group of sodomites are clerks (as distinguished from the aristocrats we will meet in the following canto). Specifically named are Priscian (a famous Latin grammarian from the sixth century), Francesco d'Accorso (a celebrated jurist from Bologna), and Andrea de' Mozzi, the one-time bishop of Florence (on the Arno) who was transferred to Vicenza (on the Bacchiglione) by Pope Boniface VIII for his unsavory lifestyle. There his "sinfully-stretched sinews" were laid to rest; this phrase is one of the only direct indications in the canto that Dante is dealing with sodomites, those who sin violently against God's nature. The time comes for Latino to rejoin his party, who are further ahead.

Notes

∴ 4–6: *As the Flemings, between Wissant and Bruges...*

The Flemings were and still are famous for their dikes. Wissant and Bruges form the western and eastern boundaries of their system, respectively.

CANTO XV: BLASPHEMERS, SODOMITES, AND USURERS

❖ 9: *before Carinthia senses the warmth*

Carinthia likely refers to a mountainous region in what is now southern Austria. "Sensing the warmth" refers to mountain snow melting.

❖ 30: *I answered, "Are you here, Sir Brunetto?"*

Brunetto Latino (more commonly Latini, d. 1294) was a poet and encyclopedist. Like Dante, he also composed an allegorical narrative poem in Italian and in the Tuscan dialect. This was probably the major source of his influence on Dante, for which he is honored here as a 'teacher,' though Dante was familiar with his encyclopedia as well. Within the poem, he refers to it as his *Tesoro* (treasure), and it came to be known as the *Tesoretto*. This is likely the work he recommends to the pilgrim toward the end of the canto (see line 119). Toynbee offers the following biography:

> Brunetto Latino, Florentine Guelf, son of Buonaccorso Latino, born in Florence circ. 1210, died 1294; he was a notary (whence the title of 'Ser' given him by Dante), and is commonly supposed (from a misunderstanding of Inf. XV. 82–5) to have been Dante's master, which in the ordinary sense of the word he cannot have been, since he was about fifty-five when Dante was born. It is uncertain at what period he began to take part in public affairs in Florence; he held an official position in 1253, and in the next year he attested, in his capacity of notary, two public documents, which are still preserved, and one of which is drawn up in his own handwriting. In 1260 he was sent on an embassy to Alphonso X of Castile (one of the candidates for the imperial crown) in order to induce him to assist the Guelfs against Manfred and the Ghibellines. While he was on his way back, he learnt from

a student who had come from Bologna, the news of the decisive victory of the Ghibellines over the Florentine Guelfs at Montaperti (Sep. 4, 1260), and the consequent expulsion of the latter from his native city...On the receipt of this disastrous news Brunetto abandoned his intention of returning to Italy, and took refuge in France. He appears first to have gone to Montpellier; he was in Paris in Sep. 1263, and at Bar-sur-Aube in April, 1264, as we know from notarial documents in his handwriting under those dates. While in France he compiled his encyclopedic work, the *Livre dou Tresor*...After Manfred's defeat and death at the battle of Benevento (Feb. 26, 1268), and the consequent discomfiture of the Ghibellines of Tuscany, Brunetto returned to Florence and resumed his share in public affairs. In 1269 at Florence and in 1270 at Pisa he acted as notary to Guy de Montfort, Charles of Anjou's vicar in Tuscany; in 1273 he was secretary to the Florentine government, and in 1275 he was president of the notarial guild; he was one of the commissioners aid guarantors of the ephemeral peace patched up between the Guelfs and Ghibellines in Florence in 1280 by the Cardinal Latino; in 1284 (Oct. 13) he was one of the two syndics of the Florentine government for the conclusion of an offensive and defensive alliance with Genoa and Lucca against the Pisans, who in the previous August had been totally defeated by the Genoese in the great naval battle at Meloria; in 1287 (Aug. 15 to Oct. 15) he served the office of prior; and in 1289 he was appointed one of the public orators of Florence; he died in Florence, aged over eighty, in 1294.[13]

---

13 Toynbee, *Dictionary*, 99.

CANTO XV: BLASPHEMERS, SODOMITES, AND USURERS

❖ 62: *who from ancient times came from Fiesole*

The Fiesole were, in Dante's time, considered the country hicks, compared with the noble Florentines who were descended directly from the Romans.

❖ 109–113: *Priscian walks along with that woeful crowd...*

Priscian (sixth century), the famous Latinist, taught grammar at Constantinople. Francesco d'Accorso (1225–1293), was a celebrated lawyer and professor of civil law in Bologna. Andrea de' Mozzi ("him whom the servants transferred") was the bishop of Florence from 1287–1295, and a White Guelph like Dante. He was transferred to the region of the Bacchiglione river, to the city of Vicenza, by Boniface VIII in 1295 for his untoward lifestyle.

❖ 122: *at Verona, race for the green banner*

The race at Verona, with which this canto ends, was typically one in which the contestants ran naked. Dante pictures Latino as one who runs and one who wins the prize of the green banner; though in reality he is way behind the others, and so is dead last.

Analysis

Much has been made of this canto, especially in our highly sexualized age where discussions and debates surrounding the sin of homosexuality have become a central part of our public discourse. It is very interesting, in that context, that there are no direct references to that particular sin in this Canto.

"Sinfully-stretched sinews", "I will come behind at your hem" (a possible double entendre in the Italian), and "all made filthy with the same worldly sin" are the only indirect references to the sin of homosexuality. While Dante obviously holds it to be a sin, and specifically a violent sin against nature, this canto focuses on different things. Specifically, Dante is interested in portraying his relationship with his former 'teacher,' in which there is great tenderness and regret on both sides.

The most famous line from this canto is probably where Dante, speaking to Latino, hearkens back to that "dear, good paternal image of you / when, in the world above, from time to time, / you would teach me how man might make himself / eternal" (lines 83–86). This is echoed and reinforced at the end of the canto when Latino desires nothing more than to be remembered in his own book, *Tesoro*, or the *Tesoretto*. In that he is content, he says. It is human nature to desire immortality, because we instinctively know we are immortal beings, and so our thoughts often take us past the day of our death; as it says in Ecclesiastes 3, God has put eternity on our hearts. C. S. Lewis famously said, and I am paraphrasing, that the reason this world isn't ultimately satisfying is because we were made for another, different world, an eternal world. Temporality has never sat well with mankind. We long for glory, and temporary glory is no glory at all. Therefore we long for that kind of immortality that makes our names remembered throughout the ages. Latino's argument here is that the door to such immortality is books. And of course this is precisely what Dante himself is doing—crafting a poem that would be published and handed down from generation to generation. This is how one achieves eternality, according to Latino.

The necessary follow up question is this: immortality to what end? What good has immortal fame given Brunetto Latino? Had he published fifty books, a hundred books, would he be any closer to true happiness in the afterlife? Dante the pilgrim must be careful here. Mere notoriety is in itself neither good nor bad; it just is. Fame can be a wonderful tool, but in whose hands and for what purpose? Fame in the hands of Latino for Latino's own ends lands him in Hell. Again, Dante must be careful. We will return to this difficulty, but for now, I leave you with this thought. Which pairing is to be preferred: anonymity and Paradise, or eternal glory and Hell? It is an ancient debate, going back, in a slightly different form, at least as far as Achilles in the *Illiad*. However, put that way, the matter should be obvious, at least in a post-Resurrection world. Paradise, no matter the circumstances, is preferable to Hell. But should no glory be sought after at all? What are we called to? It is a question that I am confident will be answered when we get to *Paradiso*, so for now I will leave it hanging. But spend some time considering and meditating on the following questions: Glory at what price? Glory for what purpose? Glory how? Glory for whom? What is glory in the first place? Why is it good?

Discussion Questions

1. Describe the topography, given the two similes at the beginning. How would this scene be staged, given the various clues in the text?

2. Given that this is the wheel where the sodomites are punished, what significance might the falling flakes of fire have?

3. Dante has been learning how to not pity the sinners, so that he might learn to fully appreciate the heinousness of the sin. But here he is full of reverence and respect for his old teacher, truly saddened to see him here. Is that a good thing? Why or why not? Defend your answer from the text.

4. Discuss the hints Latino gives regarding Dante's future. What is going on?

5. Virgil takes a back seat in this canto, with only one line. Why?

6. What is Dante up to in the final simile about the contestants in the race in Verona?

CANTO XVI

BLASPHEMERS, SODOMITES, AND USURERS

Characters

- Dante and Virgil
- Iacopo Rusticucci
- Guido Guerra, Tegghiaio Aldobrandi, Guiglielmo Borsiere

Location

- The Seventh Circle, The Third Wheel: the Blasphemers, Sodomites, and Usurers; Violence against God and His own Goods (or Nature)

Summary

Having left the first group of Sodomites, the clerks, our pilgrim meets representatives from the second group (the ones it was not fit for Latino to be with). These are aristocratic politicians, lawyers, and otherwise influential men. This is indicated, not only by their names, which we learn later, but also by Virgil's insistence that these are souls toward which one "ought to be courteous." The three that come to meet Dante, having recognized his garments, are also from Florence. It is fitting, therefore, that their conversation centers mostly on their city, and laments its increasing levels of corruption and greed. The pilgrim recognizes instantly who these three are, and pays them the reverence due to their position in society as well as to their own words and deeds. Like Latino, they are eager to rejoin their party when the conversation is complete and race back. The pair approach the cliff's edge, where the runnel from the Phlegethon that ran over the burning sands empties out into an abyss. Dante gives Virgil his belt, and Virgil throws it over the edge, apparently getting someone's, or something's, attention. It works, as the canto closes with the image of a swimmer coming back up to the surface. Like that swimmer, something is rising through the air to meet them.

Notes

∴ 38–45: *Guido Guerra was his name, and in life...*

Guido Guerra (d. 1272) was a nobleman and a Florentine Guelph, known for his daring and good sense. Tegghiaio Aldobrandi served alongside Guerra, and in a similar way. Iacopo Rusticucci was likewise a Florentine Guelph, but of a lower social rank. It is said he was driven to sodomy because of how "wild" or ferocious his wife was.

❖ 67: *Guido Guerra was his name, and in life*

Regarding the specific attribute of courtesy, important for his judgment of Florence, see the *Convivio*, where Dante says,

> And let not the wretched vulgar be deceived as to this word also, thinking that courtesy is no other than openhandedness, for openhandedness is a special form of courtesy, and not courtesy in general. Courtesy and honour are all one, and because in courts of old time virtuous and fair manners were in use (as now the contrary), this word was derived from courts, and 'courtesy' was as much as to say 'after the usage of courts.' Which word, if it were now taken from courts, especially of Italy, would mean nought else than baseness.[14]

❖ 70: *Guiglielmo Borsiere, grieving with us*

Guiglielmo Borsiere left off making purses to become a man-about-town, rubbing shoulders with the upper echelons of society.

❖ 73: *"A new people with their rapid profits"*

This refers to recent immigrants to Florence who concerned themselves more with business than with virtue.

❖ 96: *eastward, to the left of the Apennines*

The Apennines are a mountain range that cuts down through the middle of Italy, dividing it into its Western and Eastern parts.

---

14 Dante, *Convivio*, 106.

❖ 106–108: *I wore a cord wrapped tight around my waist…*
The reference to the belt with which the pilgrim *had thought / to catch that leopard with the spotted pelt* is what leads some to identify the leopard in Canto I with fraud, as the belt is being used to summon, or catch, Geryon, the beast who symbolizes fraud.

Analysis

As will become more and more obvious, the *Comedy* is a work of Christian politics just as much as it is a work of Christian theology and Christian humanism. As discussed in Canto XIV, the Church and the Empire are the twin lenses that Dante is constantly looking through. The poet's invectives are aimed equally at corrupt popes and corrupt politicians alike. And if you think about it, this makes sense. For Dante, the Roman Empire was the chosen vessel of God to be the cradle of Christianity. Therefore it was God's chosen expression of civil government, for the sake of increasing the scope of the Church's influence over the world. Thus when politicians (such as those in Florence in the late thirteenth, early fourteenth century) were bickering and fighting and turning from truth to "hubris and excess" with attention given to "rapid profits" only, there was great reason for sorrow and lament. But more than this, Florence was not just a city. It was the equivalent of a country. There was no sovereign state of Italy in the thirteenth century; there was only a sweeping collection of warring city states. Florence was a chief political powerhouse in the region of Tuscany. It was also Dante's motherland, deeply embedded into his sense of identity.

CANTO XVI: BLASPHEMERS, SODOMITES, AND USURERS

So it was for the three who come to meet him in this canto. These were Florentine nobility, from the same generation as Ciacco and Farinata, with whom the pilgrim has already conversed. In fact, in Canto VI, Ciacco mentions two of the Florentines we meet here. There, the pilgrim inquired after them, adding that they were men "who did such good." Here in this canto too, their names and good deeds are praised, both by Dante and by his generation still alive in the world above. But if they are so praiseworthy, why are they here? Ciacco's own answer to Dante's question as to where they were was, you may remember: "They are...among the souls most black" (Canto VI, line 85). Obviously good deeds and an honorable name is not enough to get you into Paradise. Friendship with the world is enmity with God. And yet, these men perhaps did accomplish genuinely good things in their time. And for that Dante is grateful. Still, it is not your best external deeds, but the object of your faith that matters most. The irony here is rich. These noblemen, highly honored citizens of a previous generation, men who are still praised in Dante's day, and likely by many of his own readers, they are found here, running around ridiculously, fruitlessly trying to avoid the burning flakes falling on the barren sand, with all the other sodomites.

This irony draws on a very real tension that is felt throughout the *Inferno*: real respect for the people Dante was grateful for on the one hand, and their eternal damnation on the other. What is going on? I want you to think about this, and offer only this thought. What might a certain level of respect for the damned accomplish (distinguishing always the sin and the sinner)? Could it be our own humility? If everyone in Hell was a Hitler, or an Argenti from Canto VIII, it would be easy in our flesh to feel superior to all these wicked, vile sinners, forgetting that but for the grace of God, there go I.

I think Dante wants us to honor what ought to be honored, to respect what ought to be respected, even in the face of an individual's denial of Christ, and refusal to repent of their sin. In this way, these two Cantos (XV and XVI), allow us to focus more on the people than on their sin, heinous though it may be, and recognize with humility the mixed nature of the human condition.

CANTO XVI: BLASPHEMERS, SODOMITES, AND USURERS

Discussion Questions

1. Why do the three souls run in a circle? And why are they compared to champions?

2. Why could Dante not join these three souls and embrace them? Why would Virgil have allowed it if he could have?

3. The three souls bemoan with Dante the loss of courtesy and valor in Florence. Why do you think that might be? Is there any irony in this given where they are being punished?

4. Come up with a theory as to why Dante says only now that 1) he wore a belt, and 2) wanted to use it to catch the leopard in Canto I. What did that leopard represent? Is there any connection here?

5. Locate and discuss the three epic similes.

CANTO XVII

BLASPHEMERS, SODOMITES, AND USURERS

Characters

❖ Dante and Virgil

❖ Rinaldo Scrovegni (Blue Pregnant Sow)

❖ Giovanni Buiamonte, the "Sovereign Cavalier" (Three Goats); Florentine house of Gianfigliazzi (Yellow/Blue Lion); the Florentine House of Ubriachi (the White Goose)

❖ Geryon

Location

❖ The Seventh Circle, The Third Wheel: the Blasphemers, Sodomites, and Usurers; Violence against God and His own Goods (or Nature)

Summary

Dante and Virgil come to the edge of the seventh circle, and, as hinted at the end of the previous canto, a gigantic monster rises up from the abyss to meet them at the top of the cliff. This is Geryon, a flying serpent with a human head and a face with the appearance of justice and kindness. This monster is the perfect image of fraud, which characterizes the sins being punished below. He lands, and Virgil approaches him to compel him to take them down to those lower circles of Hell. Meanwhile, Dante is free to briefly engage with a group of sinners he sees nearby, huddled next to the edge of the cliff. They are sitting down, though they are uncomfortable due to the heat above and the heat below. They each have an empty coin purse hanging around their necks, which they are compelled to look at for eternity. These are the usurers, those who acted violently against God by abusing God's property through financial means. He speaks with a Paduan, disdainfully stuck with a group of Florentines. After this brief interaction he returns to Virgil who has already mounted Geryon. Despite great fear and trepidation, Dante climbs up, and they begin their descent down to the eighth circle.

Notes

∴ 1–15: *"Behold there the beast with the spearlike tail…"*

Geryon, as pictured here, is Dante's own creation, though something like him appears in other texts. Regarding his relationship to fraud, see the *Convivio*, where Dante says,

> And those things which at first conceal their defects are the most dangerous; because, in many cases, we cannot be on our guard against them, as we see in the instance of a traitor who in appearance shows himself a friend,

so that he begets in us a confidence in him, and beneath the pretext of friendship he hides the defect of enmity.[15]

❖ 18: *nor were such webs woven by Arachne*

According to Ovid, Arachne challenged Minerva to a weaving duel, and won. Minerva destroyed Arachne's piece in jealousy, which drove Arachne to kill herself. See Ovid's *Metamorphoses* VI.5–145.

❖ 55–57: *that from each neck hung a purse, each bearing...*

The coats of arms seen on the purses all refer to Florentine nobility.

❖ 107: *Phaëthon let go the reins, and the sky*

Phaëthon, as told by Ovid, was the son of Helios (the god of the sun; sometimes identified as Apollo) who wanted to drive his father's chariot (the sun itself) across the sky. Helios reluctantly gives in, but Phaëthon makes a royal mess of things, and Zeus has to kill him before he destroys the earth. Icarus, son of Daedalus, famously died after flying too close to the sun with the wings his father had made. See the *Metamorphoses* II.1–328.

❖ 108: *above was blackened, as it still appears*

Though Dante here refers to the damage done by Phaëthon with a word that means cooked, blackened, or overbaked (*cosse*), sometimes translated as scorched, he is actually referring to the Milky Way. See the *Convivio*, where he says,

---

15 Dante, *Convivio*, 285.

Wherefore we are to know that concerning this milky way philosophers have held divers opinions. For the Pythagoreans said that once upon a time the sun strayed in his course, and passing through other portions not suited to his heat scorched (*arse*) the place along which he passed; and this appearance of scorching (*l'arsura*) was left there. And I believe that they were moved thereto by the fable of Phaëton, which Ovid tells in the beginning of the second of the *Metamorphoses*.[16]

Analysis

In a poem of such sweeping scope, some cantos are going to serve as narrative links more so than others. For instance, this canto provides the means of transition from middle Hell to lower Hell, from the seventh circle to the eighth circle. There is relatively little dialogue, and relatively little movement. And yet, Dante, in his genius, uses this opportunity to juxtapose two different sins in a very interesting way. The sinners in this circle are the usurers, those that lent money at ridiculously high rates of interest in order to profit off of others. They are the last of the Violent that Dante meets. But his brief conversation with the nameless Paduan wretch is placed right between extended sections dealing with Geryon, the monster of fraud. What is going on? Why would Dante sandwich the violent usurers between these two descriptions, first of the monster himself, and second of their descent on its back into lower Hell? Is there a connection?

---

16 Dante, *Convivio*, 125–126.

CANTO XVII: BLASPHEMERS, SODOMITES, AND USURERS

Interestingly, the insignias referenced all refer to *noble* Florentine families. These are not your Dickensian pawn brokers from Victorian London. They are not dirty, low class shysters. These are wealthy and noble families, with dignified reputations and gilded exteriors, much indeed like the face of Geryon. But just as the kind and just appearance of the monster does not match his cruel, serpentine body, so too these usurers, while appearing noble and grand, are really snake-like themselves, violently abusing those desperate enough to use their services. They themselves are fraud-like, though they are not actually deceiving anyone. Still, there is an incongruity between the outward appearance and the inward action. In this way, they serve as the perfect compliment to Geryon, and as the perfect transition to the circles of the fraudulent to which Dante is going.

Discussion Questions

1. Discuss where Virgil and Dante are geographically.

2. Dante gives enough clues to identify the usurers, but he refuses to name them in the text. Why might that be?

3. Is there a similarity between the usurers and Geryon? Push back on the analysis above. Could there be another reason these two are juxtaposed in this canto?

4. Discuss Dante's fear, especially in the context of his two similes referencing Phaethon and Icarus.

CANTO XVIII

SEDUCERS AND FLATTERERS

Characters

❖ Dante and Virgil

❖ Venedico Caccianemico, Jason, Alessio Interminei of Lucca, and Thais

Location

❖ The Eighth Circle, Malebolge: Fraud against those with whom there is no relationship of trust; the First and Second Ditch, the Pimps and Seducers and the Flatterers respectively

Summary

Geryon has set the travelers down at the bottom of the great cliff that separates lower Hell from the rest. They have come to the eighth circle, also known as Malebolge, or Evil Ditch. Just as the seventh circle was made up of three separate wheels, Malebolge contains ten individual ditches, wherein different kinds of fraud are punished—specifically, fraud directed toward those with whom there was no previous relationship of trust (unlike the fraud punished in the ninth, and lowest, circle). The trenches get successively lower, and rock bridges (for the most part) connect each, spanning the trenches where the sinners are punished. The travelers need to walk along the ditch until they come to the bridge. Here, within the first ditch, are two groups of people: one group walking clockwise, the other walking counter-clockwise. So it is that, as Dante and Virgil walk alongside the ditch, they walk against the flow of one group, and with the flow of the other, seeing the faces in the first group only until they cross over to the other side. All the souls are naked and are being prodded on by horned demons carrying horsewhips. In the first group, the pimps, Dante recognizes one Venedico Caccianemico, a Bolognese man who sold the Marquis de'Este access to his sister's bedchamber. They cross the bridge after a brief conversation, halting for a moment to examine the seducers walking in the opposite direction. There they notice Jason, of Argonaut fame. They keep going and arrive at the second ditch, where the flatterers are punished, submerged in excrement. Dante the poet's language turns vulgar and obscene here, in keeping with where they are. The pilgrim recognizes Alessio Interminei, a notorious flatterer. Virgil also points out Thais, the flattering prostitute from the Roman play *Eunuchus*, by Terence.

CANTO XVIII: SEDUCERS AND FLATTERERS

Notes

❖ 28–33: *like the Romans, because of the great host...*

The Jubilee referred to here was proclaimed by Boniface VIII in February, 1300. The Jubilee granted an indulgence to everyone who, confessing and repenting of their sins, visited Saint Peter's basilica in Rome.

❖ 55: *It was I who brought Ghisolabella*

Ghisolabella was Venedico Caccianemico's sister, who was sold by her brother to the Marquis d'Este (this is the "Obizzo da Este" named in *Inferno* XII.111).

❖ 61: *to say, "sipa," between the Savena*

Sipa is the Bolognese way of saying *sia*, or yes. The area demarcated here between the two rivers was so devoid of Bolognese (owing to them being in Hell), that hardly any were left who spoke the Bolognese dialect.

❖ 86–96: *It is Jason, who by heart and by sense...*

Colchis is where Jason traveled to find the golden fleece. Lemnos was an island along the way, where Jason seduced Hypsipyle, who bore him twins. Her deceit involved hiding her father, the king of Lemnos, when the men were killed by the women. Medea, the daughter of the Colchian king who loved Jason, was used to find the fleece, after which they got married. However, Jason later abandoned her for Creusa. For the probable source of these stories see Statius' *Thebaid* V.403–485 and Ovid's *Heroides* VI and XII.

❖ 116: *I saw a soul's head so filthy with shit*

The Italian word translated here (and in line 131) as "shit" is *merda*, which comes directly from Latin. In both languages, *merda* is the obscene, slang form of excrement (*sterco* in Italian, and *stercus* in Latin, used just above in line 113). Dante's use of the term is intentional and not gratuitous. Rather, his purpose is to correctly identify the disgusting vulgarity of flattery.

❖ 133: *I saw a soul's head so filthy with shit*

According to Charles Singleton, it was likely that Dante did not take the quote by Thais directly from the play *Eunuchus*, by Terence, but from Cicero's *De amicitia*, with which Dante was very familiar. The relevant portion of that work (XXVI.98–99), reads,

> Such men delight in flattery, and when a complimentary speech is fashioned to suit their fancy they think the empty phrase is proof of their own merits. There is nothing, therefore, in a friendship in which one of the parties to it does not wish to hear the truth and the other is ready to lie. Nor should we see any humour in the fawning parasites in comedies if there were no braggart soldiers.
>
> In truth did Thais send me many thanks? It would have been enough to answer, "Many." "Millions of them [ingentis]," said the parasite. The flatterer always magnifies that which the one for whose gratification he speaks wishes to be large. Wherefore, although that sort of hollow flattery influences those who court and make a bid for it, yet even stronger and steadier men should be warned to be on their guard lest they be taken in by flattery of the crafty kind.

Singleton makes the following comment: "Through his undoubted ignorance of the play, Dante has attributed to Thais the exaggerated reply ("ingentis") put by Terence into the mouth of the parasite Gnatho. In the original play this entire exchange takes place between Thraso and Gnatho, not (as Dante supposes, from an understandable misreading of Cicero, taking his "Thais" as a vocative) between Thraso and Thaïs directly."[17]

Analysis

It is interesting that this canto marks the beginning of the second half of *Inferno*, while at the same time, the pilgrim's first step into the eighth circle of Hell. It is worth noting the asymmetry: seventeen cantos covering the dark wood through the seventh circle, seventeen cantos covering circles eight and nine. Why the imbalance? The most likely reason is that the sins addressed in the final two circles were, in the medieval mind, the most serious, and therefore the most worthy of punishment. And as we will see, there are many more ways of sinning with the intellect than with the flesh. Thus there is an uneven amount of time given to these final two circles.

To reiterate the nature of Deep Hell, the sinners here were not carried away by their passions into sin; they deliberately willed their actions, in cold and calculating ways. These are the fully human sins, without any bestial lack of self-restraint mixed in. The passions do not enter into the equation. Where passions are involved, according to the medieval way of

---

17   Singleton, *Inferno*, 238.

thinking, the proportion of animal appetite to human intellect is high, making the sin "less offensive" in that it is less of an abuse of that which is uniquely human, that which uniquely bears the resemblance to the divine. To make this point again, the lustful fornicators in the second circle, though worthy of eternal punishment, have sinned on a different level than the fraudulent pimps here in Deep Hell. Their sin was merely the sin of the flesh. Here we begin to see the sins of the mind, that rational element that distinguishes us from the beasts.

We have discussed this before, and at length, but it is worth repeating: while it may be difficult for modern Christians to swallow this taxonomy of sins, I think it is helpful in at least one way. If we can agree that Hell is Hell, and that everyone here is equally separated from the life of Heaven, equally suffering under the just and holy wrath of God (remember the inscription on the gates of Hell in Canto III), then to distinguish these sins in these ways becomes instructive to us not of the afterlife, but of the nature of sin and the nature of man. That is Dante's genius, to use the images and narrative of this incredible journey in regions very distant to the living, to illustrate those aspects of the human soul and human community that are often too close for us to see.

One final point. Starting now, the language in Hell undergoes an uptick in the vulgar and obscene (especially with the Evil Claws in Cantos XXI and XXII). The use of the English word "shit" in this canto (translating the Italian obscenity, "*merda*") is intentional. And the reason is simple: flattery is disgusting and profane. It is a wicked use of the intellect, of God's gift of rationality. Remember, everyone in Malebolge (including these flatterers) is punished for fraud, the use of trickery and deceit to bring advantage to self at the expense of others. Flattery, specifically, is the calculated use of false

CANTO XVIII: SEDUCERS AND FLATTERERS

praise to achieve one's own ends. Thus, in reality, what is coming out of the mouth of the flatterers is nothing more than excrement. Their praise may have sounded golden in life, but here in the second ditch of Malebolge, it is shown for what it truly is. Again, how you live follows you into death and defines the state of your eternal suffering. Alessio and Thais have found that out the hard way.

Discussion Questions

1. Discuss (again) the fact Dante held fraud to be a more serious sin than lust, or gluttony, or even violence. Why? Are his reasons valid?

2. What is the significance in Dante employing the image of Rome during the year of Jubilee to describe the first ditch of Malebolge?

3. Why are the pimps walking in one direction, and the seducers in another? Is there meaning in the necessity of constantly seeing one another as they pass?

4. Discuss Dante's use of vulgar language in the second ditch. In what way is it appropriate? Or inappropriate? Why?

5. Vulgarity aside, what is the significance of dung with respect to flattery?

CANTO XIX

SIMONISTS

Characters

∴ Dante and Virgil
∴ Pope Nicholas III, Boniface VIII, and Clement V

Location

∴ The Eighth Circle, Malebolge: Fraud against those with whom there is no relationship of trust; the Third Ditch, the Simonists

Summary

Our pilgrim and his guide are walking along the crest between the ditches of Malebolge, heading for the bridge that takes them over the third ditch. As they make their way across, Dante sees the sinners punished there, shoved head first into holes that puncture the floor. Only their legs, from the thighs down, can be seen, with the soles of their feet completely on fire. These are the simonists, named for Simon the Magician from Acts 8. Their sin was buying and selling clerical offices. The pilgrim spies a particular pair of legs he wants to learn more about, and Virgil offers to carry him down the slope. Dante asks the soul who he is, and the soul answers in a surprising way: though he is never explicitly named, this is Pope Nicholas III, who was notorious for his nepotism. His reply to the pilgrim betrays an assumption that Boniface VIII has already died and was ready to join him in the hole. After condemning Boniface to his own same fate, he foretells that a second, more vile, shepherd will cover them both in the years to come. This third pope is Clement V, who removed the papal seat to Avignon, kicking off the infamous "Babylonian Captivity." After his death, according to Nicholas, he would join him and Boniface in the hole. After Nicholas finishes his speech, Dante launches into an invective against simony and the popes that practiced it. He is a little unsure as to whether it was appropriate or not, but is assured by Virgil's "contented aspect." Virgil then carries the pilgrim back up the hill, and they find the bridge that takes them to the fourth ditch.

Notes

∴ 1: *O Simon Magus, O wretched pupils*
Read Acts 8:9–24 for background on Simon Magus.

∴ 53: *are you standing there so soon, Boniface?*
Toynbee gives the following biography of Boniface:

CANTO XIX: SIMONISTS

Boniface VIII (Benedetto Gaetani or Guatani), born at Anagni circ. 1217; created Cardinal by Martin IV in 1281; elected Pope at Naples, in succession to Celestine V, Dec. 24, 1294; crowned at Rome, Jan. 23, 1295; died at Rome, Oct. 11, 1303...Boniface VIII, after procuring the abdication of the incapable Celestine V (see summary to *Inferno* III), secured his own election through the influence of Charles II of Naples, whose support he gained by promising to help him in his war for the recovery of Sicily...It was at the invitation of Boniface that Charles of Valois, brother of Philip IV of France, went to Florence in Nov. 1301, ostensibly to make peace between the Bianchi and Neri (White and Black Guelphs), his intervention resulting in the expulsion of the former and the exile of Dante. Boniface was thus the ultimate cause of Dante's lifelong banishment, and the poet in consequence indulges towards him a fierce hatred, assigning him, as is noted above, his place of torment in Hell while he was yet alive. It is noteworthy, however, that notwithstanding his personal hatred for Boniface Dante refuses in any way to condone the enormity of the offence committed by Philip IV in laying hands on the Vicar of Christ, when the long struggle between them, and the bitter contest with the Colonna family, finally culminated in the tragedy of Anagni. (See *Purgatorio* XX.85–96, and the summary explaining that passage.) Apart from his having prostituted the influence of the Church in the furtherance of the designs of Charles II of Naples, Boniface was repeatedly guilty of simony in advancing his own family and adherents to ecclesiastical dignities.[18]

---

18 Toynbee, *Dictionary*, 91–92.

❖ 79–81: *But already, the time my feet have baked...*

Nicholas III died in 1280. Boniface VIII would die in 1303. Thus Nicholas waited twenty-three years for Boniface to join him. Clement V would die in 1314, a period of only eleven years after Boniface. It is possible that Dante wrote this before 1314, but it is also possible that he came back to it after Clement died and touched it up. Either way, it is a remarkably bold text.

❖ 85: *He will be a new Jason, of whom one*

Singleton has the following entry for Jason:

> Jason (born Joshua), second son of the high priest Simon, wrested the office of high priest from his own brother by promising the king, Antiochus IV Epiphanes, 360 talents of silver; see II Mach. 4:7–8. Antiochus (died ca. 164 B.c.) and Jason then endeavored to root out the Jewish religion and to introduce Greek customs and the worship of Greek divinities; see II Mach. 4:13–16. This attempt led to an uprising of the Jews under the Maccabees; see I Mach. 6:1–16.[19]

❖ 87: *so with this one will France's ruler be*

The reference is to Philip the IV of France, who will favor Clement V just as Antiochus favored Jason.

❖ 92–96: *He transferred the keys into his keeping...*

See Matthew 16:19 regarding the Keys; see Acts 1:12–26 for the backstory on Matthias.

---

19 Singleton, *Inferno*, 340.

CANTO XIX: SIMONISTS

❖ 99: *He will be a new Jason, of whom one* Singleton again:

> This probably refers to Nicholas' part in an intrigue against Charles of Anjou, brother of St. Louis and king of Naples and Sicily, who had refused to marry Nicholas' niece. It was commonly believed that the Eastern emperor, Michael Palacologus, supplied Pope Nicholas with funds to aid a Sicilian rebellion against Charles that led to an insurrection known as the Sicilian Vespers and to the eventual loss (after Nicholas' death) of Sicily by the house of Anjou (see Villani, VII, 54). This was, however, only one of a number of plots and counterplots with and against the royal houses of Europe which were part of Nicholas brief career as pope.[20]

❖ 115–117: *Ah, Constantine, how not your conversion…*

Dante is referring to the legendary Donation of Constantine. See Analysis below.

Analysis

An explanation of several of the images from this canto is in order. First, San Giovanni was in the Baptistry of Florence, dedicated to her patron saint, Saint John the Baptist. This is where Dante himself, like everyone else in Florence at that time, was baptized. There is some interesting symbolism at play here. Why are the holes in which the popes are punished likened to the holes of a baptismal font? Perhaps it is

---

20 Singleton, *Inferno*, 342.

meant to underscore the new community of the damned they are baptized into. Instead of being united to the death, burial, and resurrection of Christ through the waters of baptism, they were united to their wealth, through immersion into the waters of greed and avarice. Thus they are punished in such a way as to put on display the heart of their rebellion. Adding to the baptism imagery, there is a distorted version of Pentecost happening here, with tongues of flame resting not on their heads but on the bottoms of their feet. They are indeed being baptized with the fire of the Spirit, but it is the fire of judgment, not the fire of regeneration.

Interestingly, Dante borrows the mode of execution used for professional assassins to bury his simonists. Assassins were placed in a hole head first, and buried alive. While they were there, before being completely covered in dirt, they would call for their confessor who, stooping down with an ear close to the ground, would listen to their last confession. Such is the imagery of this scene. But how are simonists like assassins? Maybe they are seen to be professional murderers of the things of God, valuing them only insofar as they bring a financial return.

Clement V is said to be a second Jason. This is the Jason from 2 Maccabees 4, who, as the second born son of a high priest, bribed the king, Antiochus Epiphanes, with silver to give him the office, ousting his elder brother in doing so. The two of them, Antiochus and Jason, deliberately attempted to Hellenize Judea, establishing Greek religious practices throughout the land. According to this analogy, not only do simonists devalue the things of God by buying and selling, they also displace true worship with false, introducing idolatrous practices, even if the artifacts of Christianity are still in use.

CANTO XIX: SIMONISTS

Dante confuses several images from Revelation in his denunciation of these papal simonists. The whore of Babylon is combined with the beast with ten horns, and is co-opted to represent the corrupt church. The seven heads and ten horns are construed as positive things, as long as "virtue" is pleasing to the "husband" (the pope). It was thought by early commentators that the seven heads were the seven gifts of the Spirit (wisdom, understanding, counsel, fortitude, knowledge, piety, and the fear of God; these were codified by Aquinas in his *Summa*) and the ten horns were the ten commandments. Thus she was born with the grace of the Holy Spirit, and guided her life by the law of God. This is what she threw away by whoring with the kings of the City of Man. This is quite a different reading of Revelation, and it would be easy to say that Dante simply forgot what John was doing. However I believe Dante was savvy enough to know he was messing with the images in a unique way. His point was to analogize Babylon (or imperial Rome, or the wicked governments of history) with the corrupt Roman church.

Finally, the "Donation of Constantine" was a legend held to be true until it was thoroughly debunked about a hundred years after Dante's death. Per the legend, believed to be authentic by Dante, the Emperor Constantine was cured of leprosy by the prayers of Pope Sylvester I. In return, Constantine gave Sylvester Rome, moving the civil seat of the empire to Constantinople. While he believed the authenticity of this exchange, Dante clearly disapproves of it, naming it as the "mother" of so many evils. Until Sylvester, the popes were committed (to various degrees) to a normal life, economically speaking. Sylvester became the "first wealthy father" and from there things only got worse over time.

At heart, Dante was a reformer. He loved the Church; as a Guelph he fought for the Church and for the pope. (The Ghibellines aligned with the political power of the emperor.) But he was not blind to her defects and atrocities. He longed to see purity restored to the papal office, and in his way (i.e. the *Comedy*), sought to expose those corruptions. This canto contains one of many diatribes against such distortions. And notice how Dante does it: he returns not to tradition first, but to Scripture, taking Nicholas back to the original relationship between Christ and Peter and the other apostles found in the Gospels and in Acts. In this he offers both a biting critique, and a constructive way forward; if only the popes would listen.

CANTO XIX: SIMONISTS

Discussion Questions

1. Read Acts 8:9–24. How does the origin story of simony compare with the abuses mentioned here?

2. Discuss the various reasons the sinners here are 1) buried head first, and 2) punished with flames on their feet.

3. What is Dante doing by having Nicholas mistake him for Boniface?

4. Examine the pilgrim's invective against simony and discuss its rhetorical power.

5. What is the relationship between the "Donation of Constantine" and the corruptions of the Church that Dante is highlighting? Is he bemoaning a certain kind of relationship between the church and the state?

CANTO XX

SOOTHSAYERS AND MAGICIANS

Characters

∴ Dante and Virgil

∴ Amphiaraus, Tiresias, Aruns, Manto, Eurypylus, Michael Scot, Guido Bonatti, Asdente, and witches

Location

∴ The Eighth Circle, Malebolge: Fraud against those with whom there is no relationship of trust; the Fourth Ditch, the Soothsayers and Magicians

Summary

The travelers come to the fourth ditch of Malebolge, where the pilgrim sees a people slowly pacing forward, as if in liturgical procession. However, upon closer inspection he realizes that this is something new and terrible—they are not moving forward, but backward. That is, their bodies are walking backwards but their heads have been twisted all the way around so that their faces are aligned with their backsides. These are the fortune tellers, diviners, and soothsayers. They attempted to look too far into the future, and so they must now always look backward, into the past as it were. They are weeping copiously; the pilgrim weeps as well, again overcome with pity at seeing the human form so distorted. Virgil criticizes him, however, for where divine justice is enacted, being right and perfect, one should not show pity (Dante makes a pun on the Italian word *pietà* which can mean both pity and piety). Pity, or compassion, after the moment of final judgment, is out of place, as it communicates a less than perfect union with the will of God. Virgil continues by pointing out several classical figures known for being diviners. Amphiaraus was one of the those that attacked Thebes (see Capaneus from Canto XIV); Tiresias was the blind prophet from Thebes; Aruns foretold the war between Caesar and Pompey; Manto was the daughter of Tiresias, taking up the family profession; Eurypylus was said (a story invented by Dante) to have divined the beginning of the Trojan War; Michael Scot was a Scottish wizard from the early thirteenth century; Guido Bonatti was a Forlian astrologer; and Asdente was a shoemaker turned prophet from Parma (hence "leather and twine"); and other witches as popularly conceived. In the middle of this catalog of figures, Virgil pauses on Manto to tell the story of how Mantua (Virgil's hometown) was founded. Interestingly, this account contradicts the account the historical Virgil gives in Book X of the *Aeneid*. Dante's Virgil even asks the pilgrim to make sure and count as fraudulent any other report he might hear, including, it would seem, the one recorded in the *Aeneid*. As he finishes, he notes that the moon is setting in the northern hemisphere, "Cain and his thorns" (or, as we would say, the "man in the moon") referring to the marks in the moon's surface. If "yesternight" was the night before Good Friday, when the pilgrim was still wandering in the dark wood, then it is now about 6am on the morning of Holy Saturday.

Notes

❖ 32: *opened itself before the Theban eyes*

Thebes was the city of Bacchus, and fell to the Seven (including Amphiaraus and Capaneus). For the story of Amphiaraus, see Statius' *Thebaid* VII.690–823; VIII.1–210.

❖ 40: *See Tiresias, that changed appearance*

For the story of Tiresias, see Ovid's *Metamorphoses* III.322–331.

❖ 46: *Aruns is he that backs up to his gut*

For the story of Aruns, see Lucan's *Pharsalia* I.584–638.

❖ 55: *Manto she was, that searched through many lands*

Manto is mentioned by Ovid (*Metamorphoses* VI.157–162), Statius (*Thebaid* IV.463–592), and Virgil (*Aeneid* X.198–200). It is in this passage from the *Aeneid* that a different account of Mantua's origin is found, one that Virgil here seems to deny (see lines 97–99).

❖ 61–66: *There lies a lake in lovely Italy…*

The frequent references to, and detailed descriptions of, actual Italian rivers, mountains, and plains, along with their castles and towns, add verisimilitude to the poem.

❖ 95: *before the folly of Casalodi*

The folly of Casalodi (the ruling family in Mantua in the 1270s), in listening to the council of Pinamonte, ended with the expulsion and murder of that family, along with almost all of the noble families that were allies with them.

❖ 108: *was an augur—when Greece was void of men*

Greece was "devoid of men" because they were all off fighting in the Trojan war.

❖ 112–114: *Eurypylus was his name; of him sings…*

The passage referred to here is the *Aeneid* II.114–124, which mentions both Eurypylus and Calchus (from line 110).

❖ 116: *in his flanks was Michael Scot, certainly*

The famous novelist Sir Walter Scott gives the following account of Michael Scot:

> 'Sir Michael Scott, of Balwearie, flourished during the thirteenth century, and was one of the ambassadors sent to bring the Maid of Norway to Scotland upon the death of Alexander III (1286). He was a man of much learning chiefly acquired in foreign countries. He wrote a commentary upon Aristotle, printed at Venice in 1496, and several treatises upon natural philosophy, from which he appears to have been addicted to the abstruse studies of judicial astrology, alchymy, physiognomy, and chiromancy. Hence he passed among his contemporaries for a skilful magician. Dempster informs us (*Historia Ecchsiastica Gentis Scotorum*, 1627) that he remembers to have heard in his youth that the magic books of Michael Scott were still in existence, but could not be opened with-

out danger, on account of the fiends who were thereby invoked...The memory of Sir Michael Scott survives in many a legend; and in the south of Scotland any work of great labour and antiquity is ascribed either to the agency of Auld Michael, of Sir William Wallace, or of the devil. Tradition varies concerning the place of his burial: some contend for Holme Coltrame in Cumberland, others for Melrose Abbey: but all agree that his books of magic were interred in 'his grave or preserved in the convent where he died.'[21]

Analysis

As Dante watches the soothsayers make their way around the ditch, he weeps, and is again criticized for overly pitying the damned. He has done this before, most notably in Canto V with Francesca and Paolo. There I defined the pilgrim's pity as an emotional sympathizing with the sinners in their pain and agony, an entering into their grievance against the laws of nature, as if they are somehow victims of anything but their own bad choices. Certainly, here, Virgil takes Dante's weeping in this way. God's divine punishment is perfect, precise, and wholly just. There is no room for "passions", no room for pity or compassion that in any way validates the sinners, or sides with them against their treatment. And if Dante is doing that here, like he most certainly was in Canto V, then Virgil would be absolutely just in his rebuke.

But is that what the pilgrim is doing? There is some ambiguity here. He tells us what he is weeping over: *when...I saw our own image so twisted round...* This striking distortion of the hu-

---

[21] Toynbee, *Dictionary*, 382–383.

man image is what grieves the pilgrim. It's possible that Virgil is right in suspecting Dante's misaligned pity. But it is also possible that he misunderstands, as the pilgrim does not say out loud what makes him weep. Only we as the reader know what he was feeling. Regardless of what is actually going on in the pilgrim, Virgil's rebuke is worth discussing: piety lives when pity is dead. Is this true? Can one pity the damned while at the same time piously rejoicing in the will of God? It bears thinking about. Certainly, pity and piety can coexist on this side of the grave. In fact they must, if the Christian mission is to advance in any meaningful way. But after death? After the sinner has made their final choice, after they have abandoned the good of the intellect, after their fear has turned into desire as they lustily pursue and embrace their punishments? Here their desires are utterly reduced to that one governing principle of self-glory and self-importance. And so aligning with the sinner here, in Hell, necessarily means aligning oneself against the Divine Might, Supreme Wisdom, and Primal Love that created Hell in the first place. So what does pity mean? To what extent does it require aligning or sympathizing with someone? Is that what the pilgrim is doing here?

If we take Dante the poet to mean that the pilgrim is only weeping at the hideous distortion he sees, then something else is going on. It is not so much pity for these particular sinners, but rather sorrow over what their sin does and has done to the human form. In this sense he is not aligning himself, however subtly, against the will of God, but rather more directly with it. In other words, what makes him weep is these sinners' attack on God's created design for man. In trying to look too far into the future, they themselves have created this situation where their heads are reversed. This would align with an interpretation of Romans 1, where judgment consists of God giving a sinner over to their own tendencies and trajectories. Dante's *Inferno* magnifies and actualizes the nature of a particular sin. God is not mocked. A man reaps what he sows. Thinking themselves as forward looking, they discover and enact here the real nature of their sin. In this sense, the pilgrim is weeping tears of horror and even righteous indignation over what the soothsayers have done in rejection of the creation order. All this is made more clear when we remember that they are frauds. They didn't actually discover anything by their own skills. They were deceived (by demons perhaps) and so deceived others. They used the intellectual gifts they had been given to corrupt others with lies and false hopes. And what that wickedness does to a person is put on vivid display.

So who is right? The pilgrim or Virgil? Well, both are. Even if Virgil misunderstands Dante's tears, his rebuke holds true. At the same time, we can stand with the pilgrim and weep at the atrocities committed against the image of God, and God's own desire for that image, training our affections to love God's will, and hate any distortion of it we might find.

Discussion Questions

1. Why do you think Dante is weeping? Is Virgil right in his assumption?

2. How does that assertion strike you, that piety lives where pity dies? How does pity change from this life to the next? Should it?

3. Why do you think Virgil spends so much time recounting the story of Mantua's origins? Is there any reason it is placed here, flanked by images of fraud, besides the presence of Manto?

4. What is the connection Dante is drawing between divination, fortune telling, the magic arts, and witchcraft?

5. How much do we know and love the will of God, specifically with regard to what that means for us as image bearers? What might Dante be wanting to teach us with regard to this?

CANTO XXI

BARRATORS

Characters

- Dante and Virgil
- The Evil Claws: Evil Tail and the rest of the Demon Party
- Bonturo Dati

Location

- The Eighth Circle, Malebolge: Fraud against those with whom there is no relationship of trust; the Fifth Ditch, the Barrators

Summary

Leaving the fourth ditch and entering the fifth, the travelers enter a place full of boiling, black pitch. After a lengthy simile conjuring up images from the shipyards of Venice, Dante brings us to a place where demons are running to and fro, plunging sinners down into the pitch and stabbing them with hooked spears when they bob back up. These are the barrators, those who swindled people out of money by means of graft and bribery. That Bonturo (Dati) is mentioned as an exemption is ironic, as he was one of the most well known mob bosses still living in Lucca at the time this was written. Here also the pair encounter the Evil Claws, a farcical collection of demons who form a mock military troop. They are crass and rude, wholly bent on mocking and tormenting the sinners in the pitch. Hiding the pilgrim in a cleft in the rock, Virgil draws their attention and their ire, demanding safe conduct. Hearing the time tested formula that "this journey has been willed in Heaven," the demons acquiesce and lead them on. However, unbeknownst to the travelers, the demons intend to play a trick on them, leading them on a wild goose chase toward a non-existent bridge. The troop with grotesque names leads them on along the boiling pitch, but not before they make a rude gesture with their tongues to their leader, a form of salute, and the leader "trumpets" the signal to start marching.

Notes

∴ 38: *look at this rector from Santa Zita*

Santa Zita was the patron saint of domestic servants, and was buried in the church in Lucca, where these barrators are from.

∴ 46–54: *The soul sank, then bobbed, its backside turned up...*

When the demons throw the soul into the pitch and he comes bobbing back up with his backside in the air, there is a disgusting blasphemy at play that isn't readily seen. The "Holy

CANTO XXI: BARRATORS

Face" was a black crucifix, made of ebony, revered especially in Lucca, the town where these barrators are from. Thus when the sinner's backside breaks the surface, not only is it black from the pitch, but it also presents a pair of "cheeks." The demons cannot help themselves from the wicked pun. This "Holy Face" must not be allowed to show itself, and they plunge it back down with their spears.

∴ 49: *Here is swimming unlike the Serchio!*

The Serchio is a river that flows near Lucca.

∴ 76: *All cried out, "Go on Evil Tail!"*

See also lines 118–123. The names of the demons are somewhat untranslatable, but an approximation is made to give the sense that the Italian gives. They are meant to be ridiculous and disgusting.

∴ 95: *negotiating to leave Caprona*

Dante himself took part in the battle of Caprona in 1289, a retaliation following the expulsion of the Guelphs from Pisa by the Ghibellines. This expulsion was the result of the events hinted at in Canto XXXIII by Count Ugolino.

∴ 112: *another five hours after this one*

"Yesterday" was Good Friday; "five hours after this one" would be about 12pm, or the sixth hour; "twelve hundred sixty six years completed since" the year 1300, looking backwards, would be the year 34 AD. At the sixth hour on that particular Friday, Jesus was nailed to the cross. He died at the ninth hour, or 3pm, but Dante here sees the process of His death as having already begun at 12pm. Therefore, even in its initial stages, His death had the power to shake Hell to pieces.

Analysis

We have seen the seriousness of sin's consequences, and we will taste their weightiness again the further down we go. But here, and in the next Canto, we get a picture of sin as a horribly destructive farce. The demons are lewd and distasteful in their vile blasphemy, and yet their antics (not to mention their names) belong on the baser stages of vaudeville. To be sure, Dante does no injustice to sin. At its core, sin is nonsense, it is insanity. This turn to low-brow comedy serves to undercut the temptation to ascribe a deep meaningfulness and dark heroism to our sinful actions. We are oftentimes tempted to cast transgression in an over-serious light, giving it a dignity that is unnatural. Certainly the effects of sin are both serious and tragic. Hell, as the center of divine judgment and eternal damnation, is no laughing matter. But what these cantos do, and do quite effectively, is to remove the pall of misplaced nobility sinners often take to themselves in defense of their own lifestyle. No. Sin is in no way noble; it can in no way be dignified. Sin is a horrible and malicious joke; it is the empty promise of a longed-for good. Sin lures a man toward gold and gives him shit instead. And the vulgarity is not only appropriate to the nature of sin, but necessary to rouse us from our complacency about what sin is. Sin is a gross and absurd deception, one that we fall for all the time. Do we really think that sin can give us what it offers? Are we really that gullible? Dante is right; only the demons are laughing.

CANTO XXI: BARRATORS

Discussion Questions

1. What does the imagery from the Venetian shipyard do in this canto? How does it compare or contrast with what follows?

2. Why does Virgil hide Dante on the bridge while speaking to the demons?

3. How is it that the demons always comply with Virgil, as soon as he pulls his "it is willed in heaven" trump card?

4. What does Jesus on the cross, and His death, have to do with the destruction of the arches?

CANTO XXII

BARRATORS

Characters

∴ Dante and Virgil

∴ The Evil Claws: Evil Tail and the rest of the Demon Party

∴ Ciamopolo, Brother Gomita, and Michael Zanche

Location

∴ The Eighth Circle, Malebolge: Fraud against those with whom there is no relationship of trust; the Fifth Ditch, the Barrators

Summary

Dante the poet opens with a lengthy remembrance of his time as a mounted soldier during the summer of 1289, in the Aretine region. He does so to make the contrast between noble military activities and the actions of the demons here in the fifth ditch (real bugles, for instance, versus the flatulence via the "novel pipe" at the end of the previous Canto). As they continue to walk with the party of demons, the pilgrim focuses his attention on the boiling sinners, who sometimes arch their backs out of the pitch hoping to find relief. This is a dangerous game, however, as the Evil Claws mercilessly skewer with their hooks those that are not quick enough, and plunge them back into the pitch. They find one such sinner in the midst of being flayed, and Dante asks Virgil to find out who it is. Though he is unnamed in the text, this is Ciampolo, from Navarre, a small kingdom in southern France. He probably committed suicide, as the illegitimate son of a scoundrel, but nonetheless is suffering here as a barrator for his activities in the king's court. Though the demons are eager to inflict pain, Curly Beard holds him apart, allowing Virgil to continue talking with him. We also hear of Brother Gomita and Lord Michael Zanche, both from Sardinia. Both of these men were deputies from the thirteenth century, and both were given to bribery. Having finished, the soul from Navarre plans a trick to escape the further torments of the Evil Claws, enticing them with the possibility of more souls to torment. As they move to their respective places, Ciampolo takes the opportunity to dive into the pitch, effectively escaping the demons, who are angry at being so deceived. This leads Bent Wing and Tread Frost into a fight in the air above the place where Ciampolo disappeared, which ends with them falling into the pitch themselves. Curly Beard arranges a rescue party, and Virgil and Dante escape before they finish fishing them out.

CANTO XXII: BARRATORS

Notes

❖ 5: *O Aretines; I have seen raiders raid*
The Aretines were Ghibellines that the Guelphs, including Dante, defeated in the battle of Campaldino in 1289.

❖ 52: *I was then one of Theobald's household*
Theobald II was king of Navarre from 1253 to 1270, known to be a just man and upright man.

Analysis

Following the opening remembrance that pits the nobility of life against the ignominy of the damned, the poet says, almost excusing his demon guides: *But when with the saints in church, or in the tavern with gluttons...* This proverb translates roughly into the more well known idiom, "When in Rome, do as the Romans do." Its use here implies that the poet considers it necessary to allow the high tenor of his comedy to dip down a couple notches. We are in the lower parts of hell after all. And so, surrounded by the Evil Claws and their infernal antics, the register of the poem slips again (following Canto XXI) into the ridiculous. The similes mirror this transition: from images of military might and gallantry, to graceful dolphins arching their backs in the sea, to frogs hiding in a swamp. But there is another aspect of this proverbial phrase. Within the proverb itself is a movement from the church to the tavern. This reflects the same movement from the third ditch to the fifth ditch, from simony to barratry. The latter is basically the civil equivalent of the former—bribes and graft and nefarious exchange of services and goods being the defining element in each. But the movement is telling.

In Canto XIV, the image of the old man in the cave on the island of Crete tells how the world and all society rests on the terra cotta right foot, which represents Christ and the Church. The left foot, made of iron, represents the civil realm. And in that image, the man, which represents humanity, rests more on the brittle right foot, than it does on the more solid left foot. What am I driving at? Humanity, even if it does not submit to her authority, finds its stability and its meaning in the Church, and not in the state. The state follows after the Church, playing what is ultimately a supporting role. In other words, like the father in a family, the Church inescapably sets the ethos of civilization. When the Church is being faithful, blessings follow, and even non-believers are grateful for the cultural capital that faithfulness produces. But this also means that when the Church is corrupt, that same corruption finds its way into society's "sanctioned" practices as well. A Church plagued with simony sets the tone for the civil realm plagued with barratry. In short, what the Church finds acceptable, society will also find acceptable.

Of course this does not mean that the unbelieving world won't always find sin and wickedness more attractive than righteousness and obedience. The human heart is bent on self, until by grace it isn't, and so will continue to push the boundaries toward deeper forms of iniquity. The world will always hate Christ, and Christ's followers. The point here is that the boundaries of a given culture, a culture in which the Gospel has taken root, are defined by where the church draws the line. At any moment in history the church has a certain amount of moral authority within the culture, directly corresponding to their courage to maintain it. But just as wicked and even absentee fathers still define the family by what they are, so too the church will always define the culture by nature of what it is. Thus, the movement from simony to barratry is not surprising. It is the natural evolution of a society where the church no longer stands against wickedness.

INFERNO READER'S GUIDE

Discussion Questions

1. What is going on in the opening remembrance? What is being contrasted?

2. Identify and discuss the various acts of fraud found in this episode.

3. What is the relationship between the Church and society? In what ways does barratry imitate simony?

4. In what way is the farcical nature of these two cantos emblematic of fraud?

CANTO XXIII

HYPOCRITES

Characters

∴ Dante and Virgil
∴ Catalano and Loderingo

Location

∴ The Eighth Circle, Malebolge: Fraud against those with whom there is no relationship of trust; the Sixth Ditch, the Hypocrites

Summary

Having momentarily gotten away from the Evil Claws, our travelers, separately, are both thinking of the same thing: how to escape this ditch and its ministers. The pilgrim voices this concern, and Virgil echoes it. Just as the devils appear, ready to do them mischief, Virgil grabs Dante and they slide down together the side of the ridge into the sixth ditch, where they meet the hypocrites. They are called a "painted people," signifying the nature of hypocrisy. They wear a physical representation of their sin as well: gold colored robes, made of lead on the inside. Their punishment is to slowly and sadly walk under the (physical) burden of their sin. Dante wants to know if there are any there of repute, and two friars overhear him speaking in his Tuscan dialect. They come over as quickly as they can—which is to say, not very. They are amazed to see him here alive, and question Dante as to who he is. The pilgrim obliges and returns the favor, questioning them. They are two friars, Catalano and Loderingo, who came from Bologna to Florence to serve as judges for a term. Each one representing a different political faction (Guelph/Ghibelline), they were installed by pope Clement IV in Florence with the stated purpose of bringing impartiality within the contentious city. Their hypocrisy is found in their efforts to violently suppress the Ghibelline party, leading to the exile of Ghibelline families in 1267. Dante begins to chastise them, but is brought up short, seeing a man crucified horizontally on the ground. This is Caiaphas, the high priest who organized the effort to put Jesus to death. The other hypocrites, as they walk in a circle around the ditch in their leaden robes, must step on him each time they pass. He, being naked, is offered no protection, and feels the full weight of every step. Virgil marvels at this, for, of course, Caiaphas had not yet died when the Roman made his previous journey down to the bottom of Hell. Virgil then asks the souls if there is another way down, as they cannot find the bridge. Catalano tells them that the bridge in this ditch was destroyed, but that up ahead is the ruin, a landslide that will lead them to the next ditch. Virgil is perplexed, as Evil Tail had said there was a bridge. Catalano reminds him

CANTO XXIII: HYPOCRITES

that the devil is a liar and the father of lies. Virgil is irritated at having been deceived, and they go on their way.

Notes

❖ 3: *as Friar Minors walk along the way*

Friar Minors was what the Franciscans called themselves.

❖ 5–6: *my thinking had turned toward Aesop's fables…*

The fable of the frog and the rat, by Aesop, referred to here goes something like this: The rat asks the frog's help to cross a river. The frog helps by tying a string to each of their legs, pulling him along as he swims. The frog then dives, to kill the rat. As the rat resists, a falcon flies overhead. Seeing the rat struggle, it swoops down and picks the rat up. The string is still tied to the frog, the frog follows, and both are eaten. The moral is that this is what happens when you intend mischief to others. Commentators are undecided as to how Dante intended this to be interpreted, but it has something to do with the Bent Wing and Tread Frost scraping together and falling into the boiling pitch. The likeliest answer is that the demons are the frog and the travelers are the mouse. The boiling pitch is the falcon. The difference being that Dante and Virgil escape, where the mouse didn't.

❖ 7: *for one cannot equate 'mo' and 'issa'*

The words *mo* and *issa* both mean *now*; the point is that their meaning is the same, though the words are different.

❖ 63: *like those that are made for monks in Cluny*
Cluny was the location of a famous Benedictine abbey in France (Burgundy).

❖ 66: *Frederick forced on some would seem as straw*
Singleton explains this reference to Frederick with a quote from the historian G. L. Hamilton:

> You must know that the Emperor Frederick II used to punish those who committed crimes against the crown in the following manner: he had a leaden cover made for the condemned man, to cover him entirely. The cover was about an inch thick. Then he had the man placed in a cauldron, and the leaden cape put over him. Then he had a fire made under the cauldron. The heat melted the lead, which took the skin off piece by piece. Finally, both the lead and the condemned man boiled. This punishment was not without immeasurable pain.[22]

❖ 103: *We were Jolly Friars, from Bologna*
The Jolly Friars were ordained as peacemaking knights, but in the end served their own pleasures instead.

❖ 108: *that it still is seen near the Gardingo*
The reference to Gardingo alludes to a section of Florence where the destruction was most severe. Hence the line, "such was our rule," is meant to convey the reality that it was an unmitigated disaster for Florence, which suffered much collateral damage.

---

22 Singleton, *Inferno*, 397.

CANTO XXIII: HYPOCRITES

Analysis

Virgil in the *Comedy* is a complicated yet fascinating figure. He is hand picked by Beatrice to help the pilgrim Dante because of his poetic abilities, the persuasiveness of his art, and Dante's love for his poetry. However, having died outside of Christ, having placed no faith in the God of the Old Testament, he is doomed to eternity in Hell. But he is pictured as one of those who dwell in the first circle, where the virtuous pagans dwell, not in torment, but in hopelessness. You will remember from Canto IV the roster of philosophers and poets and noble figures from antiquity that populated the twilit castle. On one level there is great respect given to these figures. Virgil says they are there for no particular sin, but rather because they died without baptism. This leaves the Christian with a number of questions. If Hell is judgment, what is being judged? According to Dante, what exactly is Virgil being judged for? Well, that is a tricky question, because the only answer is not given by the narrator, but by Virgil himself. But can Virgil be wholly relied upon to have a completely accurate understanding of things? He never had faith in Christ. He never saw God. He is in fact one of those whom he himself says has lost the good of the intellect. Now, the good of the intellect is to know and understand the One by whom the intellect was made, and in Whose image it exists. Virgil, by the definition of Hell, has lost this good. And so, while he retains much of his human, common-grace wisdom and virtue, he is not blessed, nor is he sanctified in any way. While he is never deceitful or wicked, he still does not have the full picture. This becomes painfully obvious even to Virgil when the travelers reach the heights of Mount Purgatory.

Here, in this Canto, the Roman shade has been cruelly tricked by Evil Tail. The limitations of his own understanding are made clear and he is angered by it. Evil Tail had said there was a bridge that crossed this ditch, when in fact it is the one place where the bridge was broken by that event that happened 1,266 years previously (the crucifixion of Jesus). But even before that revelation, he is brought up short by the crucifixion of Caiaphas. He has not seen anything like this before, and therefore marvels (*maravigliare*). Not only does this bring an air of verisimilitude to the action within the poem itself, it introduces a tremendous layer of depth and interest to the meaning of Dante's project as a whole. Virgil can only go so far. He will never be able to fully understand the judgments of God, nor grasp the whole of reality; for he has been forever denied a saving knowledge of Christ. This central and defining limitation brings a whole host of questions that are worth discussing. To what degree can we, as readers, trust Virgil? To what degree is Virgil correct in his understanding? What standard can we use to make that judgment? Does Dante benefit from his guidance? If so, how? How far can common-grace intelligence and understanding go? If Virgil says something that is true, is he right by accident (in the sense that even a broken clock is right twice a day)? Or does he have a genuine knowledge of the world that simply does not go far enough? All these questions, and more, are worth the time it takes to work through slowly and carefully. I leave it to you to do so.

CANTO XXIII: HYPOCRITES

Discussion Questions

1. Look up the fable by Aesop about the frog and the rat (or mouse). What is the connection? What is the point Dante is making in drawing the parallel?

2. Why is Virgil just as eager as Dante to escape the Evil Claws?

3. Why are the golden-colored lead cloaks the perfect picture of hypocrisy?

4. Discuss the punishment of Caiaphas. Why is he (and the others of the Sanhedrin) punished in this way, here in the circle of the hypocrites?

5. What does Catalano mean when he says Caiaphas's actions sowed "such wickedness for the Jews" (line 123)?

CANTO XXIV

THIEVES

Characters

- Dante and Virgil
- Vanni Fucci

Location

- The Eighth Circle, Malebolge: Fraud against those with whom there is no relationship of trust; the Seventh Ditch, the Thieves

Summary

At the end of the previous canto, Virgil was undeceived about Evil Tail's lie. As this new canto opens, his face is still troubled from having been deceived. However, he changes it, as quickly as frost melts away in the early spring Sun, to help Dante. They are leaving the sixth ditch via the ruin of the bridge, and the way is rough and steep. The concentric rings of Malebolge are shaped like a funnel (like all of Hell), with the walls of the ditches getting successively lower than the previous ones, though they also seem to get more difficult to climb. Thus the travelers scramble over the rocky surface, like mountaineers. When they finally come down onto the far bank, they enter the seventh ditch, where the thieves are punished. They find the ground swarming with snakes; much of the imagery here is borrowed from Lucan's *Pharsalia*. When the souls are bitten and destroyed by the snakes, they burst into flame, turn to ash, and then resume their forms like the fabled phoenix, the description of which is taken from Ovid's *Metamorphoses*. The travelers watch as this transformation happens in front of them. The sinner who undergoes the metamorphosis is one Vanni Fucci, a violent man, known to Dante, who is punished here for stealing items from the treasury of San Jacopo in Pistoia. Annoyed that he has been found out, he curses Dante, revealing something of what will happen in the coming years. The White Guelphs in Pistoia will banish the Black Guelphs, and take possession of their homes and goods. In response, the exiled Black leaders will enter Florence and take control, releasing political prisoners, and exiling the White Guelphs. Thus, Florence would change her people (White Guelphs to Black) and change her ways (her mode of government). Dante himself was a White Guelph in Florence, and the event Vanni Fucci refers to would be the occasion of Dante's own exile. This prophecy is the thief's way of getting back at the pilgrim for discovering him in Hell.

CANTO XXIV: THIEVES

Notes

❖ 1–3: *In that part of the young year, when the sun...*

The sun is in the constellation of Aquarius from January 21 to February 21; thus the image is one of late winter, when the sun melts the heavy frost.

❖ 55: *One needs to climb up a longer ladder*

Virgil could be referring either to the shanks of Satan, which they will climb to escape Hell, or Mount Purgatory, or both.

❖ 86–87: *for if she bore chelydri, jaculi...*

The chelydri, jaculi, phareae, chenchres, and amphisbaenae are different varieties of serpents referred to in Lucan's *Pharsalia*.

❖ 93: *without hope of hole or heliotrope*

The obscure reference to heliotrope comes from Pliny's *Natural History*, where he describes the heliotrope stone as having the capacity, in the right circumstances, to make someone invisible. Thus the sinners have neither the ability to escape the snakes by means of a hole in the ground, nor by becoming invisible. Singleton quotes the relevant passage:

> The heliotrope, which is found in Ethiopia, Africa and Cyprus, is leek-green in colour, but is marked with blood-red streaks...Here, moreover, we have quite the most blatant instance of effrontery on the part of the Magi, who say that when the heliotrope plant is joined to the stone and certain prayers are pronounced over them the wearer is rendered invisible.[23]

---

23 Singleton, *Inferno*, 416.

❖ 100: *Never was "O" nor "I" so swiftly scrawled*
Two letters that can be written in one stroke of the pen.

❖ 106–111: *So it is confessed by the great sages...*
For one account of a phoenix from a work familiar to Dante, see Ovid's *Metamorphoses* XV.392–402.

❖ 145–150: *Mars draws from the Val di Magra vapor...*
Singleton offers the following explanation of this obscure ending to Fucci's prophecy:

> Literally, Fucci's prophecy is as follows: Mars, god of war, draws forth from Val di Magra a vapor (*igneo* being understood), which becomes enveloped in turbid clouds. Between the igneous vapor and the clouds there shall be combat in an impetuous and harsh storm over Campo Piceno, whereupon the igneous vapor will break through the mist (i.e., the enveloping clouds) with violence.
>
> The commentators generally agree that by the "vapor" drawn by Mars from the Val di Magra is meant Moroello Malaspina, a Guelph leader who in 1288 acted as general of the Florentines in their campaign against the Ghibellines of Arezzo and thereafter held important offices in various cities. From 1301 to 1312 Morello was constantly in arms on behalf of the Neri of Tuscany, and during the campaigns of the latter against the Ghibellines of Pistoia he added greatly to his military fame.
>
> There is some doubt as to what particular battle is referred to here, since neither Villani nor Compagni makes mention of any battle on the Campo Piceno, a district near Pistoia. Some take the allusion to be to the siege and capture, in 1302, of the stronghold of Serravalle by the Florentine Neri and the Lucchese, under Moroello Mala-

spina, in the course of their attack upon Pistoia...Others hold that the reference is to the siege and final reduction, in 1305–6, of Pistoia itself by the Florentines and Lucchese, on which occasion Moroello also was a leader... Ever since the expulsion of the Bianchi from Florence in 1302, Pistoia had remained the only stronghold in Tuscany of the Bianchi and the Ghibellines. After the capture of Pistoia on April 10, 1306, the fortifications were razed and the territory divided between Florence and Luca. See Villani (VIII, 52 and 82) for descriptions of the respective battles.

It is not clear why the Campo Piceno was so called. It is at some distance from the ancient Picenum, which was a district on the Adriatic coast. As Butler and others have pointed out, the wrongful application of the name probably arose from a misunderstanding of a passage in Sallust (Bellum Catilinae LVII, 1–3) on the defeat of Catiline...[24]

Analysis

We need to once again take a step back and consider why certain sinners inhabit certain circles. From one angle, he who has broken one part of the law is guilty of breaking the whole of it (see James 2:10). So why is there not just one big circle for all "lawbreakers"? I've said this before, but it is good to remember that Dante is not writing this poem in order to hypothesize about what Hell is actually like. He is, instead, crafting a poetic theology that gives him the framework to discuss the nature of sin, the nature of sanctification, and the nature of holiness. *Inferno* is not first and foremost a representation

---

24 Singleton, *Inferno*, 425.

of everlasting damnation. It is a theology of transgression. The sinners that populate these regions are, of course, guilty of any number of actual sins, let alone given over completely to their fallen natures. But certain sins of the individuals are highlighted in order to provide opportunity to discuss what that sin actually is.

For instance, Vanni Fucci is said to be "a man of blood and great indignation." By temperament and reputation he is a violent brute. He could have easily been sent to the first wheel of the seventh circle with the others who were violent against their neighbors, or even in the fifth circle with the wrathful. Instead, Dante has placed him here in the seventh ditch of the eighth circle, where the fraudulent thieves are punished. Given that the different levels of Hell represent an escalation of perverseness, such that the sins are more heinous the further down Dante goes, the placement of Vanni Fucci brings up an interesting question: why is fraudulent theft worse than theft by violence? Why is theft by violence worse than succumbing to the passion of wrath? Again, Dante's scale of sin represents the amount of intellect involved in the sin. Since the intellect is the chief marker of the image of God upon man, to twist and pervert the intellect toward one's own sinful desires is more reprehensible than an excess of something otherwise good. The wrathful are punished where they are because they let their passions override their intellect. The violent robbers are punished where they are because their governing passions were guided in a small way by their intellect. But the thieves proper are punished in lower Hell, further down from the wrathful and the violent, because their sin was entirely intellectual. Theft proper is essentially passionless. It is pure choice, a purely intellectual decision to take something belonging to another. In Dante's taxonomy of sin, that makes theft more blameworthy, for no non-rational passions are present to mitigate the guilt.

Again, it is important not to miss the larger metaphor at work in the *Inferno*. While all sin is justly condemned and deserves death, some sins take us further and further away from God, to the extent that they become deeper distortions and perversions of the image that we bear. There are doubtless a number of different ways of talking about this reality. Dante has given us one. And the discussion is worth having, taking it for what it is.

Discussion Questions

1. Why do you think Dante opens with a simile about a peasant looking out at his fields? Does it have any relevance to the context, or is it just a random, though useful image?

2. Think through the geography of Hell; draw a rough map. What are the implications of the placement of different sinners?

3. Why might the punishment for thieves consist in being bitten by snakes and burned into ash?

4. Why is Vanni Fucci ashamed to be discovered as a thief, when his reputation was for being violent?

5. Discuss the virtues of and challenges with Dante's taxonomy of sin.

CANTO XXV

THIEVES

Characters

⁙ Dante and Virgil

⁙ Vanni Fucci

⁙ Cacus, Agnello Brunelleschi, Buoso degli Abati, Puccio Sciancato, Cianfa Donati, Francesco de' Cavalcanti

Location

⁙ The Eighth Circle, Malebolge: Fraud against those with whom there is no relationship of trust; the Seventh Ditch, the Thieves

Summary

Canto XXV opens with Vanni Fucci, in modern parlance, giving God the finger with both hands. The rude gesture known as the "fig" was made by placing the thumb between the fore and middle finger while making a fist. It had similar sexually obscene connotations to those that the middle finger has today. The defiance Fucci exemplifies becomes a microcosm for all of Hell: open hatred and rebellion against God, without hope of change or repentance. Two snakes wrap around him and shut him up, for which Dante is thankful. The sinner runs away, and Cacus the centaur rides up looking for him, carrying a load of snakes and a fire-breathing dragon on his back. He chases after Fucci, and three more souls walk up after he leaves. They look up to the bank where Dante and Virgil are standing, and ask who the travelers are. The three souls (as we find out at various lines in the canto) are Agnello Brunelleschi, Buoso degli Abati, and Puccio Galigai (called Sciancato, the gimp), all Florentine thieves. But before Dante can respond to their question, crazy things start to happen. First, a serpent with six legs (who is understood to be the Cianfa they were asking about) leaps onto Brunelleschi, wraps his legs around his body, and bites his face. Locked in this horrific embrace, the two bodies begin to merge into one. Combined in this way, they waddle off. Then, a small lizard races up to the remaining two, and jumps through the navel of Abati. Smoke pours out of his wound, and out of the lizard's mouth, mixing together. In the midst of this merging haze, the two figures begin to transform into one another: the limbs and body of the man shrink and morph into the body of a lizard, while the body of the lizard grows and expands into the body of a man. While this scene is reminiscent of Ovid, Dante self-consciously surpasses the fantastical elements in the *Metamorphoses*. The former lizard stands up, and is revealed to be Francesco de' Cavalcanti by way of the last line's reference to Gaville (the town where he was murdered, because of which Gaville suffered intense retribution from Cavalcanti's family; thus the weeping). Abati, now a lizard, scurries away, while Cavalcanti yells after him. The one remaining thief, the only one left unchanged, is finally revealed as Puccio Galigai.

Notes

❖ 15: *not even him who fell from Theban walls*

This refers to the soul Capaneus (see Canto XIV).

❖ 17–25: *I saw coming a centaur, full of rage…*

Dante takes the traditional form of Cacus, a fire-breathing half-human monster born of Vulcan and Medusa and killed by Hercules, and turns him into a centaur with a fire-breathing dragon on his back. See Virgil's *Aeneid* VIII.193–267.

❖ 95: *of poor Sabellus and Nasidius*

In Lucan's *Pharsalia*, Sabellus is bitten by a poisonous snake whose venom caused him to slowly disintegrate into a small pool of death. Again in Lucan, Nasidius was bitten by a different snake whose venom caused his body to swell into an indistinguishable mass. See the *Pharsalia* IX.763–797.

❖ 97: *Of Cadmus and of Arethusa too*

In Ovid's *Metamorphoses*, Cadmus, the founder of Thebes, was transformed into a snake as a punishment for killing a dragon that was sacred to Mars. Also in Ovid, the nymph Arethusa was turned into a fountain by Diana in order to escape the unwanted advances of the river god Alpheus. See the *Metamorphoses* IV.576–589, V.453–458, 572–641.

Analysis

The thieves' use of the intellect to fraudulently deprive fellow human beings of their rightful property is a violation not only of the eighth Commandment, it is also a trampling of the necessary trust that rests at the center of human community. All cultures, all societies recognize, to some degree, that stealing does not lead to human flourishing on a broad scale. The *Inferno*, as we have seen, bases its system of justice and retribution not directly on divine law, but rather on natural law, which nonetheless reflects the character of God. Man, made in the image of God, made male and female, was designed to live in community, in a common bond of trust and respect. In life, the thief rejects that common bond, and intentionally tramples on those relationships. Here in Hell, unrepentant thieves become permanently defined by that choice. They are surrounded by snakes and dragons as a reminder of the first serpent who encouraged Eve to steal forbidden fruit. As Satan encouraged Eve to "steal" a nature that was not her own, that is, the nature of a god, so here, snakes and dragons and lizards everywhere steal away the nature of man. Instead of gaining a higher nature through theft, the thief is brought to the lowest form of bestiality, the curse of slithering on the earth. Thieves, defined in death by their choices in life, are given over to a constant thieving of their own natures. They failed to respect the nature of others by honoring their possessions, and so here their own natures are stolen and lost, in regular metamorphoses with the bodies of snakes. This changeableness is a manifestation of their disregard for the permanent things of life, such as natural, God-given rights.

CANTO XXV: THIEVES

Discussion Questions

1. Is there a connection between theft and pride? Why is this example of Vanni Fucci's pride perhaps a fitting opening to this canto?

2. In the analysis above, I have given one possible interpretation of the presence of snakes in this ditch. What might another interpretation be?

3. Read Book IV, lines 356–388, 563–603 of Ovid's *Metamorphoses*. What are the similarities? What are the differences?

4. Dante, following Aquinas, held that the soul is the form of the body (in that the soul gives the body its definition and being). Discuss the perversion of human nature, as God created it to be, in the line, "whose forms / were ready to exchange their own matter." Why is this such a hideous punishment? And what does it have to do with theft?

CANTO XXVI

FALSE COUNSELORS

Characters

∴ Dante and Virgil
∴ Ulysses and Diomedes

Location

∴ The Eighth Circle, Malebolge: Fraud against those with whom there is no relationship of trust; the Eighth Ditch, the Counselors

Summary

Following another invective against Florence, our pilgrim and his guide leave the seventh ditch, and come to a place where they can see the inhabitants of the eighth. Here they meet the souls of Ulysses and Diomedes, the famous Greek counselors and warriors from the Trojan war. They are punished specifically for three acts: the Trojan Horse (as related by Virgil in the *Aeneid*), which opened the gate by which Aeneas was forced to flee burning Troy; the clever means by which they convinced Achilles to leave Deidamia, and his son by her, to fight in the war (as related by Statius in his *Achilleid*); and their stealthy theft of the statue of Pallas Athena (again, related in the *Aeneid*). It is worth noting that all of Dante's examples of Ulysses and Diomedes come from Roman sources, and not directly from Homer. This shapes Dante's perception of the relative merits of these Greek heroes. From Dante's perspective, they are barbarians who violated sacred Troy. Therefore, each of the examples given are interpreted as instances of fraud, deceit, and trickery. This places them in the eighth circle of Hell. More specifically, they are counselors, leading others astray through speech and rhetoric, as seen in Ulysses' story. This locates them in the eighth ditch of Malebolge. Here, sinners are consumed and hidden entirely by flame, so that no spiritual bodies are seen. Thus, only voices are heard. When Virgil asks the twin-headed flame to tell its story, it is the voice of Ulysses who tells with a tongue of fire how he came to his final end. He and his fellow sailors from of old journeyed west and passed the Straights of Gibraltar (where Hercules set up his boundary lines). Then they turned south, and sailed for five months, coming to a new land (later discovered to be Mount Purgatory). But before they can land, the new land sends a tempest that creates a maelstrom (at the pleasure of Another, that is, God) that destroys them, sending them down to their current location. On this note, the canto ends.

CANTO XXVI: FALSE COUNSELORS

Notes

❖ 9: *what Prato and the rest desire for you*

The reference to Prato, while not exactly clear, is possibly to Cardinal Niccolò da Prato, who excommunicated the citizens of Florence in 1304, after he was unsuccessful in establishing peace between the rival factions.

❖ 34–36: *As he who with the bears avenged himself...*

The youths who mocked Elisha were torn by bears. This happened shortly after Elisha witnessed Elijah ascend into heaven on a chariot of fire (see 2 Kings 2).

❖ 54: *Eteocles with his brother was placed*

Eteocles and his brother, Polycines, were born of the incestuous union between Oedipus and Jocasta. During the course of the War of the Seven against Thebes, the two brothers, who hated each other, killed one another, and their bodies were burned together. However, their rivalry continued after they died, as two separate flames rose up from the pyre, instead of just one. Hence the allusion, as the flame housing Ulysses and Diomedes spits up two flames as well.

❖ 56: *As he who with the bears avenged himself...*

For the Roman version of the events surrounding Ulysses and Diomedes that Dante was familiar with, see the *Aeneid* II.13–290 as well as Statius' *Achilleid* I.536–II, 26.

∴ 91: *When I departed from Circe, who kept*

Circe was the nymph that held Ulysses (or Odysseus) captive on her island. Gaeta, or Caieta, was named by Aeneas for his old nurse, who died in that city when they landed.

∴ 110–111: *I left Seville on my right, already...*

Seville was (and is) a city in southern Spain, marking the northern boundary of the passage, while Ceuta was a city in Morocco in North Africa, which marked the southern boundary.

Analysis

This famous, and famously debated, portion of the *Inferno* deserves the attention it has received. It is a fascinating interaction, with much left undefined, leaving the door open for much discussion. To my mind, key to understanding Ulysses is the contrast he makes with Aeneas. The Trojan exile is named once ("before Aeneas gave it that name"), indirectly named a second time ("the Roman's courteous seed"), and indirectly alluded to a third time. It is this final allusion that I find most striking, as it establishes a clear standard of judgment by which Dante condemns Ulysses to Hell. Ulysses himself says that

> neither the soft-hreatedness of a son,
> nor the piety due an old father,
> nor the debt of love which ought to have made
>
> Penelope content, could quench within
> the fire I had to become an expert
> of the world, of human vice and value.
>
> (lines 94–99)

CANTO XXVI: FALSE COUNSELORS

The contrast between this Ulysses and Aeneas is revealing, especially with regard to that central word *piety* or *pieta* in the Italian. *Pieta* comes from the Latin word *pietas* which is the key word Virgil uses to define the character of Aeneas in the *Aeneid*. Meaning "pious duty," *pietas* is what propels the Trojan refugee to fulfill his great commission of establishing the Roman world. It directs his love for his son, Ascanius; it guides his faithful duty toward his father, Anchises; it also shapes his loyalty (a loyalty which is, of course, tested by Dido) to the wishes of his wife's shade, who died in the fires of Troy, but appeared to him to tell him of his responsibility to found Troy again in Italy. In short, Aeneas understood that he was not free to follow his own desires. He had an obligation to others, to the future of his people, and therefore to the world. His submission to that obligation is the substance of his *pietas*.

By contrast (according to the Roman sources), the sweetness of Telemachus, the reverence and duty owed to Laertes, and the loyal love that ought to have been directed toward Penelope, keeping Ulysses home, could not "quench" (or conquer, *vincere* in the Italian) the ardent desire he felt to become an expert (*esperto*) of the world. In short, the obligations that bound Ulysses to Ithaca were no match for his consuming passion to know everything, to be the reigning specialist in all things human, to place the world itself underneath his own feet. He is utterly self-oriented. He cannot lay his own desires aside, and serve those for whom he is responsible. He has no *pietas*. This self-centered lack of *pietas* is what creates a space for the fraudulent counsel that leads to his own death, and the death of his companions.

This is the sin of fraud. Fraud honors no obligations except the obligation to self. Fraud loves the appearance of piety, but denies its substance. Ulysses' speech to his comrades is full of noble sentiments: with what time remains to us, he says, "do not wish to deny experience / of the unpeopled worlds beyond the sun. / Consider your fathers and grandfathers; / you were not made to live as animals, / but to seek after virtue and knowledge" (lines 116–120). This sounds noble and grand. Tennyson reinterprets this scene in his famous poem, "Ulysses" this way:

> Tho' much is taken, much abides; and tho'
> We are not now that strength which in old days
> Moved earth and heaven, that which we are, we are;
> One equal temper of heroic hearts,
> Made weak by time and fate, but strong in will
> To strive, to seek, to find, and not to yield.

At these words we all, with Ulysses' men, are supposed to stand and cheer the indomitable spirit of man. For Ulysses (both in Tennyson and in Dante), earth and heaven are mere obstacles to man's heroic heart. We will strive, we will seek, we will find, we will never yield. But a strong will is not the end of man; the beatific vision is. And that vision of God in His beauty demands we yield before Him; it demands we bow the knee in *pietas* and humility before His greater counsel. It is as if Dante foresaw the modern spirit of godless individual autonomy, and knew exactly what to do—burn it forever in Hell. It looks good on the surface, but inside it hides a self-centered and destructive will. Think of Geryon, the keeper of the fraudulent circles: beautiful face, dragonish body. This is the nature of fraud. And it is more insidious than we know.

CANTO XXVI: FALSE COUNSELORS

Discussion Questions

1. Why does Dante denounce Florence? Why does it make him sad to do so?

2. How does the reference to Oedipus' sons Eteocles and Polynices color the atmosphere of this Canto?

3. Read James 3. What is its relevance to the image of tongues of fire speaking? How does this relate to fraudulent counsel and to the image represented here?

4. According to Dante, what is bad about Ulysses' desire to know all things?

CANTO XXVII

FALSE COUNSELORS

Characters

❖ Dante and Virgil
❖ Guido da Montefeltro

Location

❖ The Eighth Circle, Malebolge: Fraud against those with whom there is no relationship of trust; the Eighth Ditch, the Counselors

Summary

As the flame containing Diomedes and Ulysses moves away, another comes up behind it, wailing. He hears Virgil dismiss the Greeks, and, recognizing the Lombard accent, stops and asks for news of his hometown. It is another flame, housing the soul of Guido da Montefeltro, a famous soldier turned Franciscan friar. Having no vision, he does not realize

Virgil is accompanied by one still alive, and assumes they have themselves recently been sent down to this ditch. Specifically, he asks whether Romagna (where he served) was at war or not. Virgil prods Dante, and invites him to respond, which he does. After a description of the political landscape, involving places known to Montefeltro, the pilgrim asks the flame to recount his own history. Afraid of infamy should his true fate be revealed, but trusting his hearers will never return to make it known, he tells his sad tale. He gave up being a soldier to make amends for his life by becoming a friar. His besetting sin was not leonine but rather vulpine. From Cicero on (see *De Officiis*, Book I), the lion (leonine) represented violence and the fox (vulpine) represented fraud, hence the analogy here. Though certainly, by some standards, a violent man, Montefeltro is punished in the eighth circle, not the seventh, for his fraudulent counsel to Boniface VIII (the "prince of a new set of Pharisees"). That final sinful act is related in the later third of the canto. Boniface had promised to absolve Montefeltro of the sin he was being asked to fall into. Believing him, Guido gave his wicked advice, and went his way. When he died, Francis came to escort his soul to Heaven (Montefeltro being a Franciscan), but a logical demon (with a logically sound argument) claimed the friar for Hell. Finishing his tale, he moves away, and the travelers continue their journey. The canto ends with the pair coming to the ninth ditch of Malebolge, where they see the schismatics, those punished for causing division ("those who earn freight by pulling apart.")

CANTO XXVII: FALSE COUNSELORS

Notes

❖ 7: *As the bull cast in Sicily*

Phalaris, a tyrant in Sicily, ordered a bull to be cast out of copper, as an instrument of deadly torture. He would punish his enemies by shutting them inside the hollow bull, and lighting a fire beneath it, roasting them alive. Furthermore, the man who actually built the bull made it in such a way that the agonizing screams of those being roasted would pass through the mouth and make the sound of a bull bellowing, as if the bull itself had been "pierced with agony." Perillus from Athens was the man who made it, and, according to tradition, was the first to be put to death within it.

❖ 41: *the eagle of Polenta broods above*

The Polenta family were Guelphs, who exercised authority over Ravenna; their crest centered on an eagle. Ravenna was where Dante settled for much of his life after his exile from Florence. Guido Da Polenta was in charge of the district in 1300; his daughter was the famous Francesca, from Canto V; and his grandson, who had the same name, was Dante's host. Cervia was a nearby town, under the authority of Ravenna.

❖ 46: *The old and new mastiffs from Verrucchio*

"The old and new mastiffs from Verrucchios" held authority in Rimini. The elder Verrucchio was the father of Gianciotto (Francesca's husband) and Paolo (Francesca's lover), also from Canto V. The idiom, making augers of their teeth, refers to their cruelty in power.

❖ 49–51: *The cities of Lamone, Santerno...*

"Lamone" and "Santerno" are rivers, on which sit the cities of Faenza and Imola, respectively. The "Little Lion of the white nest" refers to the crest of the Pagani family, who ruled Faenza and Imola in the 1290s. He ("who changes sides...") fought for both the Ghibellines and the Guelphs, depending on the circumstance.

❖ 52: *That city whose flanks the Savio bathes*

This is Cesena. In 1300 it was not ruled by any tyrant, though Montefeltro's cousin threw his weight around in the otherwise free city; thus they lived "between tyranny and freedom."

❖ 75: *That city whose flanks the Savio bathes*

For the associations of fraud with the fox and violence or force with the lion, see Cicero's *De officiis* I, 41, where he says,

> While wrong may be done, then, in either of two ways, that is, by force or by fraud, both are bestial: fraud seems to belong to the cunning fox, force to the lion; both are wholly unworthy of man, but fraud is the more contemptible. But of all forms of injustice, none is more flagrant than that of the hypocrite who, at the very moment when he is most false, makes it his business to appear virtuous.[25]

❖ 94–97: *But just as Constantine asked Sylvester...*

Montefeltro creates a parallel between himself and Boniface VIII, and Sylvester and Constantine. Boniface, like the Roman

---

25 https://tinyurl.com/3cpyankk

CANTO XXVII: FALSE COUNSELORS

emperor, was "sick" not with leprosy, but with a "fever of pride" and therefore also in need of a "physician." Montefeltro's fraudulent counsel was the medicine Boniface needed.

❖ 102: *how to raze Palestrina to the ground*

The legitimacy of Boniface's papal power hinged on the legitimacy of Celestine's abdication (see Canto III, and Celestine V who made the "great refusal"). Certain powerful families refused to acknowledge the right of Boniface VIII to be pope; he thus made war on them, on fellow Christians, instead of sending troops to the Holy Land. The most powerful of these families, the Colonna, lived in their castle at Palestrina, which was the stronghold Boniface wanted destroyed, and the reason for needing Montefeltro's counsel.

❖ 127: *he said, 'He belongs with the thieving flames'*

The "thieving flames" are not the flames of thieves, but flames that "steal" the forms of the sinners in this ditch.

Analysis

Satan is a liar and the father of lies. But he can be highly logical when it serves his ends. When he accuses us before the Father, throwing our sins in our face, he is not wrong. He lies about God's mercy and grace, and the Christian's identity in Christ. But when he asserts that our sins deserve eternal punishment, he is perfectly logical. They do, in fact, deserve that eternal consequence. And so when the black fiend denies Francis the body of Montefeltro, his reasoning is sound. You cannot repent and will to sin at the same time. If repentance means turning around and walking away from the sin, you cannot do that while simultaneously walking toward the sin. As he says, "the contradiction will not allow it!" Absolution and atonement is only effectual if repentance is genuine. You cannot be absolved of sins that you refuse to repent of. The refusal indicates a hardness of heart, the softening of which is the prerequisite of absolution. Put another way, you cannot be granted forgiveness until you ask for it, and you cannot ask for it until you truly repent of your sin. Thus Montefeltro, who, according to the story, did not truly repent but remained in the hardness of his heart, walking toward his sin while claiming to walk away from it. This lesson is a hard one, but important.

CANTO XXVII: FALSE COUNSELORS

Discussion Questions

1. Discuss the similarities between the criminals dying inside the copper bull from the simile with the souls of sinners inside the flames. What are the implications?

2. Why does Montefeltro feel free to answer the pilgrim's question?

3. What was the nature of his sin, before he became a friar?

4. Is Boniface VIII a good pope, according to Dante? Why or why not?

5. What did Boniface want Montefeltro to do? What did he promise him in return?

CANTO XXVIII

SCHISMATICS

Characters

- Dante and Virgil
- Mohammed, Pier da Medicina, Mosca Lamberti
- Ali (cousin of Mohammed), Dolcino de' Tornielli, Guido and Angiolello (elders of Fano)

Location

- The Eighth Circle, Malebolge: Fraud against those with whom there is no relationship of trust; the Ninth Ditch, the Schismatics

Summary

It is noon on Holy Saturday. Our travelers have left the eighth ditch behind, and come now to the ninth, where they find the schismatics. After the narrator offers a flourish of intentionally inadequate similes, highlighting the great number of souls that inhabit this ditch, he prepares his readers for the kind of punishment they are about to see. Here, the schismatics, those who wickedly and fraudulently divided relationships and societies, are themselves divided, chopped, and otherwise mangled. The first person Dante sees is Mohammed, the founder of Islam. Dante the poet assumed, with the majority of Medieval Christians, that Mohammed was originally a Christian who broke ranks. In this light he is a schismatic, tearing apart something that ought to have remained whole. He is graphically described as being sliced in two from his chin to his groin, and he pulls apart the two sides to demonstrate to Dante the extent of his punishment. A demon slices, cuts, chops, or in some other fashion divides each sinner; then they walk around the ditch while their wounds close up again, only to have them reopened when they return to where the demon is positioned. Mohammed asks about Dante and Virgil, assuming they are dead and are on their way further down for punishment. Virgil corrects this mistake, and reveals that Dante is actually still alive. This causes all the sinners to stop in their tracks and take notice of the odd pair. Mohammed then gives Dante a message to bring back with him to the sunlit lands.

After this, the soul of Pier da Medicina, another schismatic, also asks the pilgrim to deliver a message, this one for two elders from Fano (Guido and Angiolello) who were about to be treacherously drowned. Medicina identifies the tyrant by means of his lacking one eye; it is Malatestino of Rimini (which is the city "one here with me could wish he never saw"). Dante then asks Medicina to show him that man who wishes he never saw Rimini. The sinner does so, moving the jaw of a fellow sinner, whose tongue had been cut out. This is Curio, fellow conspirator with Julius Caesar, who affirmed the counsel that led Caesar to cross the Rubicon. This advice was given, according to Dante, at Rimini, which led to the schism of Rome, and to Curio's own punishment here in the ninth ditch.

Yet another soul, the one with his hands chopped off, asks to be remembered, one Mosca Lamberti. His counsel to revenge a certain wrong done in Florence by means of murder is said to have been the beginning of the Guelph/Ghibelline divide ("an evil seed for the Tuscan people"). His words, "The thing finished is at its end," refer to the assumption that once revenge is taken all scores will be settled. Unfortunately, though unsurprisingly, instead of ending the strife it created far more. Lastly, Dante is confronted with the appalling appearance of Bertran de Born. Allegedly, he became the counselor of Prince Henry, the younger son of Henry II of England, sowing discord and division between father and son. His confession finishes the canto, concluding with the famous word *contrapasso*, or retaliation. This is the word that describes the whole system of punishment Dante creates in Hell. As Aquinas says, "'Reciprocity' (*contrapassum*) implies a compensatory instance of being acted upon that is equal to a preceding action" (*Summa Theologiae* II–II, q. 61, 1. 4). Dante takes this definition, and expands it to mean, roughly, that sinners in Hell become defined by their sin. Their punishment, literally, matches the crime.

Notes

❖ 9–11: *of Apulia, wallowed in their blood...*

The region of Apulia is in the southeast portion of Italy, making the heel of the boot. The "long war" referred to is the second Punic War, between Rome (the Romans are the descendants of the Trojans, via Aeneas) and Carthage. The spoil of rings refers to the battle of Cannae, where the Carthaginians despoiled the Roman dead.

❖ 14: *from standing opposite Robert Guiscard*

Robert Guiscard, who we will see in Paradise, in the sphere of Mars, fought against the Saracens in the same region of southeastern Italy, in the eleventh century.

❖ 16–19: *at Ceperano, where all were liars...*

The references to Ceperano and Tagliacozzo, as well as the knight Erard, continue the theme of nasty battles fought in the Apulia region.

❖ 32: *Before me goes about Ali, weeping*

Ali was Mohammed's son-in-law and successor.

❖ 55–60: *Now tell brother Dolcino to prepare...*

The syntax of these verses in the Italian is very choppy, reflecting the chopped nature of these sinners. Fra Dolcino was a heretic from Novara in the later half of the thirteenth century, and burned at the stake along with his mistress in 1307.

CANTO XXVIII: SCHISMATICS

❧ 69: *opened his windpipe, fully vermillion*

Notice the fifth use of the adjective "vermillion", the color of the exposed windpipe of Pier da Medicina.

❧ 84: *not from pirates, nor the Argolians*

The Argolians are the people of Argos or more generally, the sea-faring Greeks. Although the reference to Neptune in the previous line also brings to mind a passage close to the end of *Paradiso* (Canto XXXIII, line 96), where Neptune wonders at the shadow of the Argo, the Argo being the ship of Jason and his crew, the first ship ever made.

❧ 90: *will they need for the winds of Focara*

Focara was a portion of the eastern Italian coast feared by sailors because of its reputation for dangerous weather. Thus prayers were made against shipwreck, prayers that ended up being useless for Guido and Angiolello, as they were drowned before they got there.

❧ 134: *understand that I am Bertran de Born*

Bertran de Born was a renowned poet; this canto is full of allusions to his poetry.

❧ 137–138: *Ahithophel did no more for David...*

Read 2 Samuel 15 for the story of David, Absalom, and Ahithophel.

❧ 142: *Thus one sees in me retaliation.*

The whole of Aquinas' response in *Summa Theologiae* II–II, q. 61, a. 4, reads

Retaliation [*contrapassum*] denotes equal passion repaid for previous action; and the expression applies most properly to injurious passions and actions, whereby a man harms the person of his neighbor; for instance if a man strike, that he be struck back. This kind of just is laid down in the Law (Exodus 21:23–24): "He shall render life for life, eye for eye," etc. And since also to take away what belongs to another is to do an unjust thing, it follows that secondly retaliation consists in this also, that whosoever causes loss to another, should suffer loss in his belongings. This just loss is also found in the Law (Exodus 22:1): "If any man steal an ox or a sheep, and kill or sell it, he shall restore five oxen for one ox and four sheep for one sheep." Thirdly retaliation is transferred to voluntary commutations, where action and passion are on both sides, although voluntariness detracts from the nature of passion, as stated above (II–II:59:3).

In all these cases, however, repayment must be made on a basis of equality according to the requirements of commutative justice, namely that the meed of passion be equal to the action. Now there would not always be equality if passion were in the same species as the action. Because, in the first place, when a person injures the person of one who is greater, the action surpasses any passion of the same species that he might undergo, wherefore he that strikes a prince, is not only struck back, but is much more severely punished. On like manner when a man despoils another of his property against the latter's will, the action surpasses the passion if he be merely deprived of that thing, because the man who caused another's loss, himself would lose nothing, and so he is punished by making restitution several times over, because not only did he injure a private individual, but also the common weal, the security of whose protection he has infringed. Nor again would there be equality of passion in voluntary commutations, were one always to exchange one's chattel for another man's, because it might happen that the other man's chattel is much greater than our own: so that it becomes necessary to equalize passion and action in commutations according to a certain proportionate commensuration, for which purpose money was invented. Hence retaliation is in accordance with commutative justice: but there is no place for it in distributive justice, because in distributive justice we do not consider the equality between thing and thing or between passion and action (whence the expression 'contrapassum'), but according to proportion between things and persons, as stated above (Article 2).[26]

Analysis

In responding to Mohammed's mistaken assumption about Dante and Virgil both being dead, Virgil says, "to give him a full experience / he must needs be led by me, who am dead, / through this Hell here below from wheel to wheel…" It is a good reminder both to Dante and to us, his fellow travelers, of why we are here. Why must we witness all this horrific suffering and punishment? Why must we wade through all the various forms of *contrapasso* that define the different circles and wheels? It is so that Dante, the man lost in a dark wood, having strayed from the right way through too much spiritual sleepiness, may gain full experience (*esperïenza piena*) of the manifold consequences of sin. To recover the right way, to be able to ascend the ladder of the stars, and reach his true end, the beatific vision, he must first understand, and

---

26 https://www.newadvent.org/summa/3061.htm#article4

experience, the nature of misdirected love. All sin is disordered love: too much love (concupiscence), too little love (violence), or intentionally misdirected love (fraud). And it was into this realm that Dante was on the verge of entering permanently, having abandoned the right way. Mercy redirected his steps, but not away from the experience of consequence. Rather he is brought into the experience itself, though protected; for he is not yet dead, and is still a pilgrim passing through. In this way, he is able to see first hand, to taste the bitterness of where sin leads, and what an unrepentant sinner becomes in the fullness of Hell. He witnesses first hand, before it is too late, and while it may still do him good, what it means to lose "the good of the intellect."

We have come across this specific word for experience (*esperïenza*) twice before. In Canto XVII, in the third wheel of the seventh circle, before they descend to lower Hell on the back of Geryon, Virgil encourages Dante to speak to the usurers, "So that you may take / the fullest experience (*esperïenza*) from this wheel…" (Canto XVII, 37–38). And it is meant in much the same way as it is here, that Dante may gain from the interactions the experience needed to understand more fully the nature and character of sin. But interestingly, it is also the word used by Ulysses in Canto XXVI, when the famous traveler is stirring the souls of his shipmates to join him on one last adventure. He encourages them: "do not wish to deny experience (*esperïenza*) / of the unpeopled worlds beyond the sun" (Canto XXVI, 116–117). Much ink has been spent comparing Dante and Ulysses, and their different journeys. Of interest here is the fact that experience by itself is not bad. Ulysses was eager for as much experience as was humanly possible, and then some. And in so far as he yearned to experience and to know, he was not in sin. Experience and the desire for experience is essential to the creation mandate, calling men and women to take dominion of the earth. Where Ulysses fell was in grasping after experience, rather than submitting to the boundaries of natural and divine law. Dante, by contrast, is being given this experience by Virgil, and, ultimately by God Himself, for the sake of his reclamation. It is not an experience Dante would have chosen, but it is one that he needs; it is not one he is grasping after, but one that he receives. Like Ulysses, he too will come to the shores of Mount Purgatory. But unlike Ulysses, his entrance will be granted, for he comes along the proper path.

Here in Hell, the pilgrim is given a special dispensation to experience the consequences of action. Through his narration, we too experience what sin is and where it leads. The question that has yet to be answered, but will be addressed in the following canticles, is this: experience to what end?

Discussion Questions

1. Describe the connection between schism and the punishment suffered in this ditch.

2. In what sense is Mohammed understood to be a schismatic?

3. Based on what you know so far about Dante, why do you think Curio is here among the schismatics, but Caesar is in limbo with the virtuous pagans?

4. "The thing finished is at its end": Mosca thought that he could end a cycle of violence through murder, that once that was done, all strife would be at an end. Instead, it ended in an even greater divide between citizens and cities. What might Dante be saying? Is a thing finished ever fully at an end? In what way does an action live on after it has been completed?

5. Define *contrapasso*. Discuss different examples of this principle that you have seen thus far.

CANTO XXIX

FALSIFIERS

Characters

∴ Dante and Virgil

∴ Griffolino, Capocchio

∴ Geri del Bello, Albero of Siena, Stricca, Niccolò, Caccia d'Asciano, Bartolommeo de' Folcacchieri (*il Abbagliato*)

Location

∴ The Eighth Circle, Malebolge: Fraud against those with whom there is no relationship of trust; the Tenth Ditch, the Falsifiers

Summary

It is now 1pm on Holy Saturday. The pilgrim's eyes are drunk with all the mangled mayhem of the ninth ditch. He is intoxicated by the blood and gore. Virgil has to rebuke him and remind him that there is more to see, and time is running short. Dante defends himself, saying that he was looking for a relative he believes is suffering there. Virgil affirms that the relative, Geri del Bello, was indeed there, and was motioning violently to Dante, but Dante did not see him. They move on and come to the rim of the tenth and final ditch of Malebolge. As they walk over the ditch, the travelers see the falsifiers, including the alchemists, who attempted to transform, among other things, base metals into gold. In this way they "aped nature" by their art, fraudulently passing one metal off as another. They are portrayed here as sickly, weak, and full of scabs. Unable to sit up on their own, they prop themselves up in pairs, back to back. Dante and Virgil come across a pair of Italians, Griffolino and Capocchio. Griffolino tells the amusing tale of how he died, after lying to the gullible Albero, who was the son of the bishop of Siena. Dante then remarks on the general stupidity of the Sienese, to which Capocchio responds, arguing that there were a few clever Sienese: Stricca, Niccolò, Caccia d'Asciano, and Bartolommeo de' Folcacchieri (il Abbagliato, or the Bedazzled), as well as Lano from Canto XIII. All these men were part of a club, called the Spendthrift Club, whose members were bent on gaining a reputation for living large and extravagantly. Capocchio lists some of their good qualities in their defense. Nevertheless, he too is against the Sienese, especially as it gives him an opportunity to reveal himself to Dante. Capocchio was a fellow student with Dante, one who had a talent for mimicry. But here, his face is full of scabs, and so Dante must "sharpen [his] eye" and look hard in order to recognize him. Like Griffolino, he was burned at the stake, but he died for his practice of alchemy.

Notes

❖ 10: *Already, the moon is beneath our feet*

The moon is beneath their feet, which means the sun is above their heads; thus it is shortly after noon, or around 1pm.

❖ 28: *Geri del Bello. You were so wholly*

An early commentator (Benvenuto) included this note on Geri del Bello, the first cousin of Dante's father:

> This Geri was a nobleman, brother of Messer Cione del Bello degli Alighieri. He was a troublesome and factious man, and he was murdered by one of the Sacchetti, nobles of Florence...because he had sown discord among them. His death was not avenged for about thirty years. Finally, the sons of Messer Cione and the nephews of this Geri took their revenge, for they killed one of the Sacchetti in his own house.[27]

❖ 29: *captivated by him that held Hautefort*

Hautefort was Bertran de Born's castle.

❖ 46–49: *Were all of the ill from the hospitals...*

During the later middle ages, the valley of the river Chiana (Valdichiana) was known as a place where malaria was rampant, especially during the summer months.

---

27 Singleton, *Inferno*, 529.

❖ 59–66: *in seeing people so sick in Aegina...*

Aegina was the island off the coast of Greece named for the nymph Aegina, one of Jupiter's many mistresses. According to Ovid, Juno took revenge on the nymph and on her island by killing almost all of its inhabitants by plague. But then, responding to a request from his son (by Aegina), Jupiter transformed the ants of the island into people. These became the Myrmidons, from the Greek for "ant." (See *Metamorphoses* 7.523–657.)

❖ 76: *Never yet have I seen a curry comb*

A curry comb was a metal comb used to groom horses' manes.

❖ 116: *for not making him Daedalus, he had*

For the tragic story of Daedalus and his son Icarus, see Ovid's *Metamorphoses* VIII.200–235.

Analysis

Blood and gore have long possessed an addictive quality. Augustine said, in his *Confessions* (6.8): "For when he saw that blood, he drank cruelty in with it and did not turn away, but he fixed his sight on it and drank in fury unaware and he took pleasure in the wickedness of the spectacle and became drunk [*inebriabatur*] with pleasure in blood" (Durling, Note to Canto XXIX). While Dante is not exactly rejoicing in the spectacle, indeed he is ready to weep, there is a certain fascination in him that Virgil must confront. In doing so he reminds Dante that there is a purpose greater than any specific sight. As discussed in the previous canto, Dante is being led through Hell to gain a full experience. In this canto, Virgil again says that he is leading his charge in order to "show him Hell." It follows that any undue lingering on one part could lead to a misunderstanding of the whole. Readers of the *Inferno*, and the *Comedy* as a whole, would do well to remember this exhortation. It is easy, with Dante, to fix our gaze on one aspect of the suffering in Hell that the poet depicts, to the exclusion of all else. Part of Dante's genius is to captivate the mind with images so preposterous and at the same time so real and tangible. This mythological realism draws us in, almost giving us a presence with the travelers as they go down and down and down. Four times thus far Dante has identified his audience as members of the party, calling us his readers. It is an identification that gains in significance as the *Comedy* progresses. In this way, Virgil's rebuke of the pilgrim can be a rebuke for us as well. We need to remember that something greater than any one canto, or any one image, is going on. The significance of the moment must always be located within the significance of the whole. We are here as pilgrims too, in need of the full experience, and what that full experience alone can teach. What that lesson is, we will see. But the reminder is relevant: "the time that is granted us is now short, / other things have been given you to see / that you have yet to see" (lines 11–13).

Discussion Questions

1. Why does his relative's actions make Dante feel more pious (or charitable) toward him? Is this a good thing?

2. Dante covers his ears when he hears the laments, saying that they are like arrows that have been made out of pity. Why does he cover his ears? Is he right to do so? Why or why not?

3. Why are the damned always enthralled to see Dante?

4. What is the relationship between alchemy and fraud?

5. Why are these particular falsifiers pictured as sick and scabbed? How is that a fitting punishment for alchemy?

CANTO XXX

FALSIFIERS

Characters

- Dante and Virgil
- Griffolino, Master Adam
- Gianni Schicchi, Myrrha, Potiphar's Wife, Sinon the Greek

Location

- The Eighth Circle, Malebolge: Fraud against those with whom there is no relationship of trust; the Tenth Ditch, the Falsifiers

Summary

This canto opens with another epic simile, using the violence and grief of both Thebes and Troy (stories taken from Ovid's *Metamorphoses*) to provide a baseline against which to compare the far greater violence of two particular wretches here in the tenth ditch of Malebolge. They are Gianni Schicchi and Myrrha, who run around thrashing the other sinners. Both were impersonators: the first impersonated his deceased uncle, Buoso Donati, for financial gain (the gaining of a prize mule); the other impersonated her mother to incestuously gain access to her father's bed. While the alchemists suffered from sores and lesions, the impersonators suffer from rabies. After Griffolino finishes telling the travelers these stories, the pilgrim looks around at the others and sees the enormous shade of Master Adam, who suffers from a form of dropsy (known today as edema) that severely increases his thirst, swells his belly from improper digestion, and makes his face boney and thin. Thus, were it not for his legs, he would look just like a lute. Master Adam, we learn, minted counterfeit coins. He practiced his art in Romena, near Florence, where he forged coins stamped with the image of John the Baptist. Next to him lie Potiphar's wife, who falsely accused Joseph of rape, and Sinon, the Greek who lied to the Trojans about the nature of the wooden horse that was being led into the city. Sinon and Adam get into a testy and insulting (though, admittedly, somewhat humorous) back and forth, which enthralls Dante just as the gore of the previous circle "inebriated" his eyes. Virgil, again, has to rebuke him (and maybe his readers as well?) for being so captivated, and Dante is ashamed. Virgil closes the canto with the reminder that the desire to hear such debased conversation is a base desire.

CANTO XXX: FALSIFIERS

Notes

❖ 2: *because of Semele, was set against*

Semele, the daughter of Cadmus, the founder of Thebes, bore Bacchus to Jupiter. Juno, to exact her revenge for Jupiter's infidelity, convinces Semele to ask Jupiter to see him in all his glory. Jupiter is loath to do so, knowing what would happen, but agrees anyway. He appears to her as the god of thunder that he is, and accidentally strikes Semele with lightning, killing her.

❖ 4: *Athamas was driven mad, so much so*

Athamas loved Semele's sister, Ino (adulterously of course), and had two sons by her. These are the "wife" and sons he mistook for a lioness and cubs, after Juno (possibly in revenge against Ino, who nursed Bacchus) caused him to go mad.

❖ 16: *Hecuba, a sad wretch taken captive*

Hecuba, wife of Trojan king Priam, was the mother of Polyxena and Polydorus (as well as Hector, Paris, and the rest). After they were taken captive by the Greeks, Polyxena was sacrificed on the tomb of Achilles, who was her betrothed (see notes to Canto V). Following this, Hecuba saw her son Polydorus cast up onto the shore dead, full of the wounds he suffered from the wars. She therefore went mad, and was transformed into a dog. These three stories (Semele, Athamas, and Hecuba) are all from Ovid's *Metamorphoses*.

❖ 31: *The Aretine was left, trembling, and said*

The Aretine is Griffolino.

❖ 86: *even though it circles eleven miles*

In the previous canto, Virgil told Dante that the ninth ditch was twenty-two miles in circumference (XXIV.9); this ditch is exactly half, coming in at eleven miles in circumference. This is interesting, especially as it would mean a bridge spanning the ditch would need to be at least a half mile long!

❖ 97: *one is the false accuser of Joseph*

For the story of Joseph and the false accusation of Potiphar's wife, see Genesis 39:1–20.

❖ 98: *the other is Sinon, false Greek of Troy*

For the story of Sinon and the Trojan Horse, see *Aeneid* II.13–290, lines 148–149 specifically

Analysis

Master Adam tells Dante that he is plagued with visions of the area in which he falsified the coins. It is a beautiful picture of green hills and rivers, which are presented to him as part of his punishment, in that they increase his thirst. After describing this idyllic landscape, he admits that he longs to see at least one of the brothers who encouraged him to mint counterfeit coins. He believes at least one is already dead and there with him in Hell, but cannot move to look for him because of his weight. But he wants vengeance so badly, he would rather see them suffer in Hell, than gain access to the Fonte Branda, a famous spring, which would, of course, relieve his thirst. Notice what Dante the poet is doing here. We

CANTO XXX: FALSIFIERS

know at least a few general things about the damned: 1) they are not good, 2) they have lost the good of the intellect (that is, the desire to see God), 3) they are bitter and hateful, and 4) they prefer personal vengeance and satisfaction to their own redemption and relief from suffering. Master Adam, suffering intensely from thirst, would rather forgo any relief that a spring might bring, if forgoing meant catching sight of his former friends in pain. What is more, even if he could only walk one inch every hundred years, he would spend that time searching all 5.5 square miles of the trench (eleven miles long by .5 miles wide) for the brothers. Like his namesake, he would turn his back on the Edenic water of life, for the sake of his own twisted desires.

What is Dante telling us? To be damned is to shift all the way to one side of the continuum. In life we struggle through a spiritual war in which our base passions and desires fight against reality and the image of God. For believers, the transforming power of the Spirit gives us victory over these passions and desires, as we grow in the ability to say no to our flesh (something Dante is still learning to do as well). But for those without the Spirit, those who continue to live in the flesh, as Master Adam did, they are only constrained in this life from being wholly given over to their lusts by the grace of God poured out on the just and the unjust alike. Reality and the image of God constrain wickedness to a certain extent, bringing shame intended to lead to repentance. But in death, when that restraint is taken away, and the lost sinners lose the influence of that common grace, they are left with nothing but their own shriveled souls. There is not the least hint of a desire for anything good. Notice how the image of repentance pops up in the coin stamped with John the Baptist. Notice also how it has no weight with Adam. There is neither sorrow, nor repentance, nor shame. There is only the desire for vengeance, to see one's enemies suffer more than oneself. It is an attitude that is as bad, if not worse, than the physical mauling of others that occurs throughout the circles of Hell. Whatever tears we have seen along the way, they are not tears of remorse, but tears of anger and of spite.

In short, Hell is where all falsifying, of every stripe, is exposed and undone. Hell is where the sin one thought they could get away with is discovered to have been known all the time, with the justly commensurate punishment awaiting those that do not repent. In Hell, the weight of common and restraining grace is removed, and the sinner is left with nothing but themselves and their self-consuming bitterness and hate. It is described in this work by Dante not for our entertainment, but as a warning—a lesson Dante the pilgrim continues to learn. To want to watch such filth play out is a base desire. The purpose of the full experience is not to scratch an infernal itch, but to transform the desires, and reorient the habits toward truth and beauty and goodness.

CANTO XXX: FALSIFIERS

Discussion Questions

1. Discuss the impact of the epic similes, and the role they play, both in the poem and in our understanding of the action.

2. Discuss the relationships of alchemy and scabs, impersonators and rabies, and false minters and dropsy (in other words specific forms of falsifying and their punishment).

3. What are the similarities between Master Adam and where he lived and our first father Adam and Eden? Is there a purpose behind the similarities?

4. What is the impulse in us to see another suffer, even at the expense of some benefit to us?

5. What is the significance of Dante feeling shame in Hell while the sinners around him have ceased to feel any shame at all?

CANTO XXXI

THE RING OF GIANTS

Characters

∴ Dante and Virgil
∴ Nimrod, Ephialtes, Antaeus

Location

∴ Transition to the Ninth Circle, the Ring of Giants

Summary

The travelers have made it through the first seven circles of Hell, and all ten ditches of the eighth circle, Malebolge. Now they approach the final circle. But just as they needed Geryon to help them down from the seventh circle to the eighth, so now they need help getting down to the very bottom of the great abyss they have been descending. The eighth and the ninth circles are separated by a steep cliff, and standing around the inside of that rim are giants, both the Nephilim from Genesis and the monsters of Greek mythology. Their feet stand somewhere near the bottom (see line 17 of the next Canto), but they are visible from the waist up from the final edge of Malebolge. As the pilgrim peers through the darkness, he understandably mistakes them for towers of a new city. Virgil explains his error, and Dante is filled with fear. The first giant they see is Nimrod, the founder of the tower of Babel. (Genesis 10; the poet Dante is here assuming that Nimrod was one of the giant Nephilim, though this is not actually confirmed by any text in Genesis.) The distance from his waist to his shoulders measures around twenty to twenty-five feet, far more than three tall Frisians standing on each other's shoulders could reach. With a head the size of Saint Peter's pinecone (an actual bronze relic in Rome), his upper half would be somewhere in the neighborhood of forty feet. Guessing that his legs are roughly the same length, Nimrod stands around eighty feet high. His brief outburst, "Raphèl maì amècche zabì almi," is intentionally nonsensical: because he caused the multiplication of languages at Babel, he is denied the gift of intelligent speech. Next they pass by Ephialtes, son of Neptune, who with his brother attempted to build a mountain high enough to throw down the gods from Olympus. After this they come to Antaeus. As the son of Earth, he gained his strength by maintaining contact with the ground. Hercules came to end his tyranny and pillage, and did so by lifting him off of the ground, thus making him weak and able to be crushed by Hercules's strong grip. Other monstrous giants are mentioned (Briareus, Tityos, and Typhon) who either attacked or violated the gods in some way and were condemned to Hell for their outrages. Virgil asks Antaeus to give them a hand down to the lowest pit of Hell, Cocytus, which is a frozen lake of ice. Antaeus agrees and sets them down. As the giant bends over to set them down on the ground, Dante is reminded of a specific leaning tower in Bologna.

Notes

❖ 4: *so I hear that the spear of Achilles*

A legend grew around the power of Achilles' spear to heal the wounds it inflicted.

❖ 17–18: *when Charlemagne lost the holy exploits…*

The "holy exploits" (Italian: *santa gesta*) of Charlemagne and the tragedy of Roland are sung about in *The Song of Roland*, the most famous of the literary form *chanson de geste* (Old French for "songs of heroic deeds").

❖ 40: *for, as the walls of Montereggione*

Montereggione was a castle, northwest of Siena, that was surrounded by fourteen large towers.

❖ 77: *this is Nimrod, by whose evil planning*

Nimrod is first mentioned in Genesis 10:8–11. For the story of the Tower of Babel, see Genesis 11:1–9.

❖ 94–96: *this is Nimrod, by whose evil planning*

The war of the Titons, of which Ephialtes was one, is summarized in Horace's Odes, III, iv, 42–52, which reads:

> Full well we know how the impious Titans and their frightful horde were struck down with the descending bolt by him who rules the lifeless earth, the wind-swept

sea, cities, and the gloomy realms below, who alone with righteous sway governs the gods and throngs of men. Mighty terror had been brought on Jove by that insolent crew bristling with hands, and by the brothers who strove to set Pelion on shadowy Olympus.[28]

❖ 99: *of the immeasurable Briareus*

Briareus, son of Uranus and Gaia, was one of the giants that fought against the gods. Virgil describes him as having a hundred arms and fifty heads (*Aeneid* Book X.565–568).

❖ 100: *To which he said, "You will see Antaeus"*

Singleton gives this brief biography: "Antaeus, the son of Neptune and Earth, was a mighty giant and wrestler of Libya, invincible as long as he remained in contact with his mother, Earth. Hercules discovered the source of his strength, lifted him from the ground, and crushed him while he held him so (see Lucan, *Pharsalia* IV.593–660)."[29]

❖ 108: *Ephialtes was quick to shake himself*

Ephialtes is upset to be described as less fierce than Briareus.

❖ 114: *a good five ells worth, subtracting the head*

Five ells equals roughly twenty-five feet.

---

28 Singleton, *Inferno*, 574.
29 Singleton, *Inferno*, 575.

∴ 115–117: *"O you that, in the fortunate valley…"*

"[T]hat fortunate valley" along the Bagradas River (in Tunisia) is where Scipio beat Hannibal in 202 BC, leading to the end of the second Punic War.

∴ 124: *Do not make us try Tityos or Typhon*

Tityos was a giant born to Jupiter and Elara, and killed by Apollo and Diana for the attempted rape of their mother, Latona. Typhon was a monster born to Gaia and Tartarus, who also attacked Olympus, and was killed by Jupiter. In a passage from the *Pharsalia*, Lucan implies that Anteaus is more powerful than Briareus, Tityos, and Typhon (*Pharsalia* IV.593–597).

Analysis

The narrator, after praising nature for ceasing to make such horrible brutes (mercifully limiting herself to elephants and whales), says: "for where the faculty of the mind joins / an evil will and power to itself, / there is no refuge that mankind can make" (lines 55–57). The same principle Dante is touching on can also be described this way: the brighter the angel, the darker the demon. In other words, the more glorious, strong, and beautiful something is, the worse it will be if it turns evil. Thus Satan, originally the brightest and most beautiful of the angels, becomes the most evil and treacherous of the demons. In other words, an evil will corrupts a creature in proportion to that creature's original capacity for goodness. The giants pictured here, were corrupted by an evil will. That wickedness, combined with giant strength in a rational creature, becomes the kind of creature bent on assaulting Heaven (or Olympus) itself. And the principle is worth remembering, as it translates into our own experience. Man was created in God's image and endowed with rationality and intelligence. We were placed in this world to tend it, cultivate it, protect it, and steward it, to the glory of God our Maker. And, when we live in harmony with our created purpose, by grace, oriented toward God in obedience, we can do great good in this world. When we sin, we step outside of that created purpose. But sin does not erase the ability to do great things. Rather, it twists those great things into greater levels of destruction. Every man, woman, and child has a responsibility before God to obey Him, and live according to their created purpose. Furthermore, everyone is given various capacities, gifts, talents, and abilities (see Matthew 25:14–30), and the goal is to use those gifts to bring a return for good. But when an evil will enters in, those talents get squandered. Each of us has a responsibility to use our gifts and talents and capacities for good (and good as defined by Scripture); and each of us has the ability to bury those talents in the ground. The point here is that the greater the capacity, the greater the scope one's effect on the community will have. One talent squandered, while enough to condemn the wicked servant, will not have the same kind of societal impact that five talents squandered would have. And so, those to whom a greater number of talents have been given, whether that is realized as a national/international audience, a successful corporation, or a place of influence over cultural or subcultural norms, they also have the added responsibility of exercising those talents for good, not only for themselves, but for the downstream effect that good will have on others. For the greater the influence, the greater the tyranny will be if those responsible

CANTO XXXI: THE RING OF GIANTS

nurture an evil will. These are the Dantean Giants, bestowed with tremendous strength and power, and with rationality. But their evil will transformed them not into petty, small-minded criminals, but rather the fierce and arrogant destroyers of civilizations, who, in their pride, attempted to scale the walls of Heaven itself.

Discussion Questions

1. It was said that Achilles' spear could heal the wounds it inflicted (See Ovid, *Art of Love* Book IV, 43–48). In what way is this simile appropriate to what Dante has experienced at the end of the last canto?

2. Find and discuss all the descriptions of the giants as towers.

3. Why is Nimrod's punishment a fitting one? How about the punishment of Ephialtes?

4. Fame, Virgil says, is the thing that is longed for in Hell. What is the significance of that description? How does this desire for fame goad Antaeus into reaching out "in haste"?

CANTO XXXII

CAINA AND ANTENORA

Characters

❖ Dante and Virgil

❖ Camicion de Pazzi, Bocca degli Abati

❖ Alessandro and Napoleone de' Alberti, Mordred, Focaccia (Canni de' Cancellieri), Sassol Macheroni, Buoso da Duera, Tesauro de'Beccheria, Gianni de'Soldanieri, Ganelon

Location

❖ The Ninth Circle: Fraud against those with whom there is a relationship of trust; Caina and Antenora, treachery against kinsman and country, respectively

Summary

The travelers have at last arrived in the ninth and last circle of Hell. It is the fourth river of the underworld, Cocytus. However, in Dante's conception it is a frozen lake at the very center of the earth, that place toward which all rocks (Earth itself) and all weight (what we know as gravity) thrust down. This is where the traitors are punished, those who committed acts of fraud against friends and family, people with whom the fraudulent were in a relationship of trust. Cocytus is divided into four concentric rings: Caina (traitors against kinsmen, named for Cain, from Genesis 4); Antenora (traitors against one's country, named for Antenor from the *Illiad*); Ptolomea (traitors against guests, named for Ptolemy, governor of Jericho); and Judecca (traitors against lords/benefactors, named for Judas Iscariot). This canto depicts only the first two sections.

After leaving the giants behind, the travelers walk out onto the surface of the lake, and the pilgrim notes the thousands of heads poking up out of the ice. An unnamed sinner warns him not to step on their heads. As he gets closer, he notices that their teeth are all chattering (like "storks") and their faces have turned purple, both results of the cold. They come upon a pair of sinners, tightly clasped in each other's arms under the ice. The pilgrim asks who they are, and they look up to answer, but the unfallen tears in their eyes drip down as they move their heads and instantly freeze over their eyes, prohibiting them from seeing. They turn to each other and begin smashing their heads together. Another sinner nearby gives enough information for the pilgrim to know who they are: Alessandro and Napoleone de' Alberti, two brothers who killed each other over their inheritance. The informative sinner also points out Mordred, King Arthur's traitorous relative; Focaccia, who killed his cousin; and Sassol Mascheroni, who also killed a relative. He then reveals himself as Camicion de Pazzi, another treacherous kinsman murderer. Carlino, a relative of de Pazzi, will commit the slightly more heinous crime of treachery against one's country or party. Thus Pazzi's name

CANTO XXXII: CAINA AND ANTENORA

will be "cleared" because his relative will do something more wicked, landing him in the next section of Cocytus.

As the travelers leave, making their way toward the center, they enter Antenora; Dante accidentally (or not?) kicks a sinner in the face. Based on what that sinner says about Montaperti, Dante is intrigued and wants to know who this is. (Montaperti was a famous Guelph/Ghibelline battle, where after much bloodshed, the Guelphs, Dante's own party, were defeated. This is the battle referred to in *Inferno* Canto X.85–86. The sinner refuses to name himself, so Dante gets in his face and starts pulling his hair, demanding that he talk. As the sinner reacts to this treatment (by barking) another sinner starts complaining of the racket and reveals his name. He is Bocca degli Abati, a Ghibelline and a traitor who feigned sympathy with the Guelphs and then betrayed them at Montaperti. After Dante discovers who he is, he lets go, promising to bear news of his fate to the world above. Abati goes on to reveal the identities of others who are nearby: Buoso da Duera (the one who outed Abati), another Ghibelline, who was bribed by the French into treachery; Tesauro de'Beccheria, an abbot who was beheaded for helping the Ghibellines after they had been exiled from Florence; Gianni de'Soldanieri, a Florentine Ghibelline who turned Guelph and thus turned against his own party; Ganelon, the stepfather of Roland (from *The Song of Roland*), who accepted a bribe from the Saracens to betray Charlemagne and the French; and Tebaldello, a Ghibelline who helped the Guelphs to a victory by secretly unlocking the gates of the city of Faenza. As the travelers move on, they come to a particularly (and famously) gruesome sight: another pair of sinners, one of whom is devouring the brains of the other. This canto ends with Dante making a deal with the one devouring, to find out who he is and the story behind his current actions.

Notes

❖ 11: *Amphion great aid in walling up Thebes*

Amphion, son of Jupiter and Antiope, built the walls of Thebes. With the aid of the Muses, playing his lyre, he magicked stones down from Mount Cithaeron, which formed the walls. See Horace's *Ars Poetica*, lines 394–396, which reads,

> ...hence too the fable that Amphion, builder of Thebe's citadel, moved stones by the sound of his lyre, and led them whither he would by his supplicating spell.[30]

❖ 16–18: *As we were down in the dark reservoir...*

There is an interesting anomaly, in that the previous canto made it seem the giants were standing on the floor of the ninth circle. Here, the travelers are "quite a bit deeper than the giants' feet." Make of it what you will.

❖ 25–30: *The winterly Danube in Austria...*

"The winterly Danube" does not freeze over as hard as this ice. The Don was a river in Russia, considered the boundary between Europe and Asia. Mount Tambura and Pania della Croce are peaks of the Apuan Alps.

❖ 88: *The winterly Danube in Austria...*

Toynbee offers the following note on Antenor:

> The name of this division is derived from the Trojan Antenor, who was universally, in the Middle Ages, held to have betrayed Troy to the Greeks...The Homeric ac-

---

30 Singleton, *Inferno*, 583.

count, that he tried to save his country by advising the surrender of Helen, was apparently lost sight of at that time. There is no hint of Antenor's treachery in Virgil.[31]

❖ 103–104: *"...a thousand times." I was twisting his hair...*
Nehemiah 13:25 reads,

> And I contended with them, and cursed them, and smote certain of them, and plucked off their hair, and made them swear by God, saying, Ye shall not give your daughters unto their sons, nor take their daughters unto your sons, or for yourselves.

❖ 130–132: *Not otherwise did Tydeus gnaw on...*

Statius records that Tydeus, one the seven kings that fought against Thebes, was mortally wounded by Menalippus, a Theban. Before he died Tydeus killed his killer, and in his death throes, started gnawing on Menalippus' head, through the bone and into the brain. See the *Thebaid* VIII.739–762.

Analysis

In Canto XX, Virgil tells Dante that "Here piety lives when pity is dead. / Who is more impious than the one who / reacts to divine judgment with passion?" (Canto XX, 28–30). It is a striking exhortation, one that at first seems mean-spirited. Shouldn't we pity the damned in their suffering? As we considered back there, Virgil's question reminds us of the implications of pitying the damned: pity in some way means

---

31 Toynbee, *Dictionary*, 37.

emotionally siding with the sinner in judgment, which in turn means standing in judgment over the divine will. True piety therefore means withholding compassion from the damned, in such a way that contrasts with the compassion we show toward unbelievers who are still alive. I rehash this here, because it makes sense of Dante's actions toward Bocca degli Abati. Dante the pilgrim takes violent action (both by kicking his face and pulling out his hair) which is called by Abati, "punishment / for Montaperti." It is an intriguing episode that confronts us with the reality of the consequences of sin, and what our response to that judgment should be.

On the one hand, God takes no pleasure in the death of the wicked (see Ezekiel 18:32, 33:11). Judgment, therefore, is free from any sort of malicious vindictiveness. There is no pleasurable delight in meting out the consequences of sin. At the same time, those consequences are real and necessary. In Hell, the punishments we have seen constitute a final "giving them over to their impurities," a "giving them up to their dishonorable passions," and a "giving them up to a debased mind" (Romans 1:24–32). Hell is God giving sinners over to themselves, entirely through the ultimate withdrawal of His common grace and mercy, and sustaining life. It is where they have lost, forever, the good of the intellect, which is to know and love God. Virgil's (and thus Dante's) point is that to show pity to someone in this state of final and everlasting judgment is to do something even God has stopped doing. It is to take on a "holier-than-God" attitude that ultimately cultivates a diminishment of one's hatred of sin. In Hell, the damned are so identified with their sin that they become nothing more than their sin. This is the idea behind *contrapasso*, or righteous retaliation. Therefore, to pity the damned, really, is to pity the sin. This is the lesson Dante the pilgrim begins to learn only

CANTO XXXII: CAINA AND ANTENORA

after he swoons with pity for Francesca and Paolo. Their story floods him with compassion and pity, but it is an impulse that he must learn to control, as he discovers with greater clarity the nature of the damned. To pity Francesca is to diminish her guilt, which is to cast aspersions on the divine judgment. Which, obviously, one should not do. Dante is learning what it means to side with God in all things. Here in Hell, he is learning to side with God concerning the nature of sin. In the following canticles, that lesson will take on new and different flavors, but the goal is the same.

And so, with regard to Bocca degli Abati, Dante's actions are consistent with the nature of punishment experienced by the traitors of the ninth circle. They have violated every natural bond through their treachery and abuse of the intellect, and so are undeserving of even common courtesy. Dante, of course, could restrain from action as a show of grace, as he does elsewhere, but that does not mean his actions here are out of line. He is merely entering into the judgment already pronounced. He is learning a proper hatred for sin. Everything that made Abati a fitting object of compassion and pity, a figure whose inherent dignity was centered in being an image bearer of God, has died. All that is left is the sinful nature, and nothing more. Dante's actions are directed, therefore, toward that gnarled root of bitterness and treachery, not toward the image bearer who once was alive in our world.

Discussion Questions

1. What is the thrust of this canto's opening lines, and invocation of the muses ("those women")?

2. Why is there a lake of ice in the center of Hell? What might the ice signify?

3. Consider the order of treachery: against kinsman (Caina), country (Antenora), guests (Ptolomea), and lords/benefactors (Judecca). Dante's overarching point throughout the *Inferno* is that sins deepen in heinousness the deeper one goes down. Thus, what is the significance of this order?

4. Discuss the reticence of some sinners to reveal themselves, and the readiness of all to tattle on their companions.

CANTO XXXIII

ANTENORA AND PTOLOMEA

Characters

- Dante and Virgil
- Ugolino, Brother Alberigo
- Archbishop Ruggiere, Branca Doria

Location

- The Ninth Circle: Fraud against those with whom there is a relationship of trust; Antenora and Ptolomea, treachery against country and guests, respectively

Summary

The soul who is eating the head of another soul, having heard the pilgrim's request at the end of the previous canto, raises his mouth and wipes it clean on the other's hair. He then begins his tale. He is Count Ugolino, and the sinner he is feasting on is Archbishop Ruggiere. The reason he is here in Antenora is briefly passed over; to Ugolino, it doesn't matter nearly as much as the reason he is taking his own vengeance on Ruggiere. Instead, he goes on to describe his own final days and those of his four sons (Anselmuccio, Gabbo, Uguiccione, and Brigata—somewhat fictionalized here in his story as very young children, given their "tender age"). He has a dream in which he imagines Ruggiere hunting him with three Ghibelline families, as if he were a wolf with his cubs. In the dream, Ruggiere's hounds find the "father and his sons," and tear them to pieces. He awakes to the sound of his children also dreaming, but dreaming about bread instead. After they are all awake, they hear the sound of the tower being nailed shut, a sign that they will no longer be receiving food. Slowly, and agonizingly the children die, and Ugolino, stricken by grief, but even more so by hunger, eats their remains. After he finishes his story, he returns to his present meal, the head of Ruggiere.

Dante, on hearing this tale, curses the city of Pisa for being so heartless as to allow the four children to suffer in such a way ("on such a cross"), calling the city a "Thebes reborn," attaching the name of Pisa to that of the ancient city which was known for its cruelty and bloodshed. The two travelers move on into the Ptolomea, where betrayers of guests are punished. Here, instead of being forced to hold their faces down their heads are thrown back. This means that the tears in their eyes are frozen immediately. They have "visors of crystal" and cannot see. Dante's own face is stiff with cold, and yet he still feels a breeze on his skin. He thinks this is unusual, as they are at the center of the Earth, where "every vapor…is spent." He asks Virgil, who tells him he will soon see where that wind comes from.

As they walk along, a soul, thinking they are destined for Juddeca, asks them to remove the ice as they pass by so that he can find even just a moment of relief. Dante strikes a bargain: if he reveals who he is, Dante will help; if the pilgrim fails, he will "condemn" himself to keep going into the very center of the ice. This is, of course, something that he is already committed to doing, so he does not intend on keeping his end of the bargain. But the sinner cannot know this, and so falls for it. He is Brother Alberigo, who was a Jovial Friar (like Catalano in Canto XXIII). He belonged to a Guelph family in Faenza. He betrayed, and ordered the murder of Manfred, a close relative and influential Guelph leader. Alberigo invited Manfred and one of his sons over for dinner. Meanwhile, he had given a group of assassins the code phrase "bring the fruit" at which point during the dinner they would come and murder the guests, which they did. The "evil fruit" of Alberigo became something of a catch phrase after this, and finds its way into the depiction of the friar here. Now in Hell, he has been given the "date" of punishment for the "fig" of his treachery.

Alberigo hopes to further ingratiate himself to the pilgrim by ratting out his neighbor, one Branca Doria, who murdered Michel Zanche (see Canto XXII), also at a banquet. But of more interest to the pilgrim (and to us) is the discovery that both Alberigo and Doria are actually here in Hell, because the pilgrim happens to know that they are still alive (at the time of this journey, in the spring of 1300). As Alberigo explains, when someone betrays and murders a guest his soul is immediately cast into Hell, while a demon inhabits his body for the remainder of the days allotted to him. Thus the bodies of Alberigo and Doria are animated by demons in the world, while their souls suffer punishment in the third portion of the ninth circle of Hell. Following this, the pilgrim condemns the Genoese, just like he condemned the Pisans, for cultivating such barbarous and inhospitable people.

Notes

∴ 1–75: *Raising his mouth from his ghastly repast...*
The reason Ugolino is here should be remembered. Antenora is that section of Cocytus where traitors against one's country or party are punished. Ugolino, originally a Ghibelline, switched sides when it became politically expedient to do so. During the back-and-forth between the two parties during the later half of the thirteenth century, Ugolino took power in Pisa. He was joined by his grandson, Nino Visconti, a Guelph (also a friend of Dante's, whom we will meet in *Purgatorio*). Nino eventually grew strong enough, however, to become a rival. Ugolino (as a Guelph) conspired with the leader of the Ghibellines, Ruggiere, to help drive Nino out. He left Pisa while this happened, but when he returned, he found that Ruggiere had betrayed him as well, and seized his political office. With the help of prominent Ghibelline families (such as the Gualandi, Sismondi, and the Lanfranchi—see Ugolino's dream) Ruggiere falsely accused Ugolino of betraying Pisa (and their castles). It is after this that Ugolino and his children (in reality, two grown sons and two (maybe even three) grandchildren, one as old as fifteen (this will become important in the analysis below) are imprisoned and starved to death. Thus, both of these souls are in Antenora because they betrayed their party affiliates: Guelph Ugolino betrayed his Guelph

CANTO XXXIII: ANTENORA AND PTOLOMEA

grandson Nino, and Ghibelline Ruggiere betrayed Ugolino, after he had returned to the Ghibelline party.[32]

❖ 9: *you will see me speak and weep together*

Note the similarity between Ugolino words here ("see me speak (*parlar*) and weep (*lagrimar*) together"), and Francesca saying, "I will recount, as one who weeps (*piange*) and speaks (*dice*)" (Canto V, line 126). Though different words are used, they are synonyms (*lagrimar* and *piange*; *parlar* and *dice*) and they allow for a nice resonance between Ugolino and Francesca. (Also note the similarities between lines 4–5 here and Canto V.121–123.) I think Dante is using the lustfulness and lack of self-restraint exhibited in Francesca to add color and depth to Ugolino's lust for vengeance. Just because he is in the lowest circle, having sinned entirely with his intellect, does not mean he is above wonton desires. He is eating the head of Ruggiere, after all. Like Francesca, he has clearly been taken captive by base desires.

❖ 80: *of the beautiful land where sì is said*

That is, Italy.

❖ 124: *before the goddess Atropos snips thread*

For the story of the Ptolemy for whom this section of Cocytus is named, see 1 Maccabees 16:11–17, which reads,

> Ptolemy, son of Abubus, had been appointed governor of the plain of Jericho, and he had much silver and gold, being the son-in-law of the high priest. But his heart be-

---

32 Singleton, *Inferno*, 608–609; taken from an account by the fourteenth-century historian Villani.

came proud and he was determined to get control of the country. So he made treacherous plans to do away with Simon and his sons. As Simon was inspecting the cities of the country and providing for their needs, he and his sons Mattathias and Judas went down to Jericho in the one hundred and seventy-seventh year, in the eleventh month* (that is, the month Shebat). The son of Abubus gave them a deceitful welcome in the little stronghold called Dok which he had built. He served them a sumptuous banquet, but he had his men hidden there. Then, when Simon and his sons were drunk, Ptolemy and his men sprang up, weapons in hand, rushed upon Simon in the banquet hall, and killed him, his two sons, and some of his servants. By this vicious act of treachery he repaid good with evil.

∴ 126: *before the goddess Atropos snips thread*

Atropos was one of the three fates, the one in charge of snipping the thread of a person's lifespan. The other two, Clotho and Lachesis, oversaw the starting and continuing of a person's life, respectively.

Analysis

Ugolino is one of the three most famous characters of the *Inferno* (Francesca and Ulysses being the other two). His story is graphic and full of pathos. It grabs our sympathies by the throat and forces us to feel the injustice of the situation. No one can read this story, and not feel indignation against the Pisans for "crucifying" the little children the way they did. The pilgrim himself is enraged, and wants the whole city of

CANTO XXXIII: ANTENORA AND PTOLOMEA

Pisa drowned in consequence of their actions. But what if something else is going on? What if that rage is precisely what Dante the narrator wants us to feel in order to subtly expose a deeper impulse at work? One reads this story and immediately is drawn into sympathy with this traitor being punished in the deepest circle of Hell. Why does Ugolino so nonchalantly pass over his own sins, and immediately fixate on the horrendous crime that was done to him? And why does he intentionally fictionalize the event? Dante the poet knew the historical grandson, Nino, who was betrayed; he knew the story first hand; he knew that Ugolino was imprisoned with two fully grown sons and two (maybe three) grandsons which were not of a "tender age." So why does Dante's Ugolino change history? And furthermore, why does he get indignant with those who are not weeping at his story? Especially when he himself never wept, and even now is not weeping?

These questions present a fascinating look at how Dante the poet engages his readers and leads those willing to look at the problems square in the face into a deeper understanding. When we first encounter the Count, he is busy munching away on the brains of Ruggiere, his betrayer. When the pilgrim asks his question, he lifts his head, and takes the time to wipe his mouth. This is not a man stricken with grief. The horrific action we witness is deliberate. Though captive by base desires (see above), he is not wild or out of control. He is polite about his task. He then tells a fictionalized and sensationalized account of what happened, in which Ugolino postures himself as the victim. In looking away from why he is in Hell, he tries to justify his current act of revenge. What other choice does he have, than to eternally eat the brains of his betrayer? His vengeance is just, in his eyes, and he wants us to side with him: "But what you cannot have heard, you will hear, / that is, how cruel my death was, and whether / he has done me injury, you will know" (lines 19–21). But throughout his narrative he reveals just how much of a victim he is not. First, in his dream, he characterizes himself as a hunted wolf, which should remind us of the she-wolf way back in Canto I (standing for avarice), who would be hunted by the greyhound. Second, not once does he give his sons any words of comfort or consolation, though they speak comfort to him. And third, he underscores the fact that while his sons were weeping, he never wept once, having been turned to stone. Fourth, while he wants the pilgrim to understand and validate his decision to eat his dead children's bodies, the fact remains that that is what he did. Truly, he has used his children throughout his story to gain sympathy, to vindicate himself, and to draw others into justifying his actions; he has cannibalized them in more ways than one to advance his own agenda. This is not a noble father, despite his sentimental narration.

What Dante seems to be doing is highlighting the reality that sinners will do anything to justify themselves, to deflect any blame, and to assume the status of victim. After reading Ugolino's account, and doing so in a superficial manner, we move on forgetting that he himself is a betrayer of his own party and kin, the sin for which he is suffering in this portion of Cocytus. We are conditioned by Ugolino to only remember what a horribly cruel death this was, and feel bad for them all. But he himself is a liar and a traitor, and, having died in his sins, has now become the full realization of that sin, and therefore deserves none of our pity, which the pilgrim refuses to give. Notice in his invective against Pisa, it is only concerning the innocent children that he is so upset. His sympathy is entirely for them, with none left over for Ugolino. Even though he likely knew the true history, and the true ages of the sons (and grandsons), he runs with the fictionalized version Ugolino tells because it doesn't substantially change the charge against Pisa—they still killed innocent sons for the sake political advantage, for which the Archbishop is justly punished here as well. Once again, we are reminded that we cannot trust what the sinners in Hell say. While they may say true things, they do not speak truth. They have collapsed entirely into themselves, and can only speak from that twisted perspective. They are not interested in upholding the beauty and rightness of true justice. Instead, they only seek self-aggrandizement, in whatever form they can find it. With Dante we should learn to be on our guard, not only against the self-justifications of others, but against our own fictionalized justifications as well.

INFERNO READER'S GUIDE

Discussion Questions

1. Discuss Ugolino's account. On first reading, how does it make you feel? Sympathetic to the Count? More bitter against the Archbishop? Do you notice how he has drawn the attention away from his own sin?

2. Twice in this canto, the narrator castigates a city and its inhabitants, first Pisa, then Genoa. Is he justified in doing so? What is his purpose?

3. Is there any significance to the fact that in the first two sections of Cocytus the faces are turned down, and in the third section, the faces are turned up? Why might that be?

4. Discuss the punishment of tears freezing in the eyes, turning further tears into an instrument of pain as they well up in the socket, under the veil of ice.

5. What is the "advantage" of Ptolomea? Why do you think this special, and highly interesting, exchange is saved for the particular sin punished here?

CANTO XXXIV

JUDECCA

Characters

∴ Dante and Virgil
∴ Lucifer, Judas Iscariot, Brutus, Cassius

Location

∴ The Ninth Circle: Fraud against those with whom there is a relationship of trust; Judecca, traitors to lords and benefactors

Summary

Our travelers have finally reached the center of the abyss. The pilgrim steps into the final section of Cocytus: Judecca, where the betrayers of lords and benefactors suffer. All the souls here are thoroughly submerged beneath the ice in various positions—all except three. When Dante and Virgil stand before Satan (also known as Dis, the one for whom the city of Dis is named), Dante feels like he is undone. "I did not die, nor did I stay alive," he says. He is standing at the center of the entire universe, at the point furthest from God, before a giant monster. The first thing the pilgrim notes about Satan is his sheer size: the height of the giants they just left (Nimrod, etc.) doesn't even compare to the length of Satan's forearm. If the giants are somewhere around seventy to eighty feet tall, that might put Satan's forearm at about ninety feet long, which means he is enormous—perhaps in the neighborhood of 250 feet tall, though only a third of him is seen above the ice. Furthermore, the fallen angel has three giant heads, each with a mouth eternally chewing a sinner. In the middle mouth, Judas Iscariot is punished for betraying Jesus. In the two mouths on either side are Brutus and Cassius, the primary betrayers of Julius Caesar.

After taking in this gruesome spectacle for a quick minute, Virgil tells Dante that it is time to go. The pilgrim hops on the Roman poet's back, and they start climbing down Satan's hairy side. Interestingly, it seems the ice comes up to his hair, and not all the way to his skin, for there is space enough (between the tufts of hair) for the travelers to climb down through the ice. They start around the middle of his chest and climb down the side of his stomach. When they get to his hips, the very center of his body, and thus the exact center of the earth/cosmos, Virgil reaches down to the hair just beyond his feet, and pulls himself up. He then starts to climb upwards. Dante is thoroughly confused. When they get just a bit further on, they come to an open cavern and a ledge. Virgil places Dante on the ledge, and then joins him, stepping off the hairy legs of Satan. Dante is bewildered. He had expected to see Hell again, since they were climbing up. But instead he sees the devilish legs, reaching up to Satan's feet. What has

CANTO XXXIV: JUDECCA

happened? They have, of course, crossed through the center point of gravity.

They are now in the southern hemisphere, climbing up to the opposite side of the world, which means that time has shifted back twelve hours. They arrived at Judecca at nightfall, around 6pm; it takes them about an hour and a half to reach the ledge where Dante asks his questions, which would put them at 7:30pm in northern hemisphere time. But now that they have crossed the center of the earth, the clock has moved back by twelve hours, meaning that it is 7:30am of the same day (Holy Saturday), which is what is meant by mid-tierce.

Here, something of Dante's mythos has to be explained. In this poetic construct, when the world was made, God put dry land in every region of the globe. When Satan fell from Heaven (read Isaiah 14:12–15), he fell at the exact opposite spot from what would become Jerusalem. However, the land that was there, fearing this fallen angel, fled down into the ocean, and pushed its way up into the land under the future Jerusalem, thus raising the level of the middle east. Satan therefore fell through the seas and into his tomb, where he was lodged at the very center. More earth, which was surrounding the place where Satan fell, also fled; but that bit of land fled upwards, out of the water and into the air of the southern hemisphere, leaving the "natural cellar" the travelers find. This second displacement of land, as we will discover in the next canticle, is what formed Mount Purgatory.

The travelers climb up a small canyon carved by a little stream, perhaps from the river Lethe on top of Mount Purgatory. It would be fitting for the memory of sin washed away in that river to be taken down here to Hell, but Dante nowhere discusses that clearly. They climb up and finally out, finally seeing the stars. Interestingly, all three canticles end with the word *stelle*, or stars. This is the defining movement of the story, and we too are well on our way to see the stars

Notes

⁘ 1: *"Vexilla regis prodeunt inferni"*

These words are typically left untranslated since they are in Latin, and not Italian. (I include the translation as a footnote.) It is the first stanza from a sixth-century hymn by Venantius Fortunatus, sung during passion week. The full first verse is as follows:

> Abroad the regal banners fly,
> Now shines the Cross's mystery;
> Upon it Life did death endure,
> And yet by death did life procure.[33]

⁘ 39: *There was one in front, and that vermillion*

Notice the last use of the adjective "vermillion", the color of the central face of Satan.

⁘ 45: *who come from that place whence the Nile flows down*

These are the Ethiopians; hence the color black.

⁘ 46: *Beneath each face extended two great wings*

Singleton notes that Satan "has kept the six wings which he had as a seraph, but now they are monstrously joined to the

---

[33] Singletone, *Inferno*, 626.

three necks instead of being as Isaiah had seen them."[34] See Isaiah 6:2, which reads,

> Above it stood the seraphims: each one had six wings; with twain he covered his face, and with twain he covered his feet, and with twain he did fly.

❖ 100–105: *"Before I uproot myself from this void..."*

There seems to be some slight irritation in Dante the pilgrim's voice, annoyed not so much at Virgil, but at the state of confusion he is in.

❖ 121: *Beelzebub as his tomb is pushed out*

See Isaiah 14:12-15, which reads,

> How art thou fallen from heaven,
>   O Lucifer, son of the morning!
> how art thou cut down to the ground,
>   which didst weaken the nations!
> For thou hast said in thine heart,
>   I will ascend into heaven,
> I will exalt my throne above the stars of God:
> I will sit also upon the mount of the congregation,
>   in the sides of the north:
> I will ascend above the heights of the clouds;
>   I will be like the most High.
> Yet thou shalt be brought down to hell,
>   to the sides of the pit.

❖ 128: *Beelzebub as his tomb is pushed out*

Beelzebub is another name for Satan.

---

34 Singleton, *Inferno*, 630.

❖ 138: *the beautiful things conveyed by Heaven*

The phrase *cose belle*, "the beautiful things," is used both in line 40 of Canto I, and in the second to last line here in Canto XXXIV, forming a nice inclusio:

> the sun above was mounting with those stars
> that were there together when Love divine,
> for the first time, moved the beautiful things;
>
> (Canto I.38–40)
>
> we climbed upwards, he first and I second,
> until I saw, through a round opening,
> the beautiful things conveyed by heaven.
> Then we came out to see again the stars.
>
> (Canto XXXIV.136–139)

❖ 139: *We then came out and saw once more the stars.*

All three canticles end with the word *stella*, or stars, emphasizing the upward trajectory of the entire poem.

Analysis

For the student of Milton, nothing could be more different from *Paradise Lost* than Dante's portrayal of Satan. As we have seen, there is something clownish about Dante's prime devil. He is not the crafty, internal, melodramatic fiend of the English epic. No. Here, he is simply a monstrous, dim-witted ogre. In fact, the further into the description of Satan we get, the more we realize how imbecilic he actually is. His three mouths are crunching sinners, yes, but they are drool-

CANTO XXXIV: JUDECCA

ing constantly as well. His chins are a mess of tears, spit, and blood. His hairy shanks serve as a ladder to the travelers. His six bat-like wings keep flapping, but have become the very instrument by which Cocytus remains frozen. He is the ultimate epitome of self-consumption; he is an idiotic oversized clown. He is the buffoonish Evil Claws writ large. For all his (literal) centrality, very little time is actually spent on Satan. Which is purposeful. Sin is emptiness; pure evil is almost a nothingness. For evil is parasitic, it corrupts the good. And only the good has real substance. Take away that substance, take away the good presence of a good God, and His good grace, and what you are left with is a demented overgrown bat monster, making his own prison, dripping in his own bodily fluids. He is a mess. There is nothing more to say. He is simply not interesting. He is so far from light and goodness and joy, that Virgil can hardly wait to keep going. And neither can we.

Discussion Questions

1. Why, do you think, are the sinners completely submerged in Judecca?

2. What is your first impression of Satan? Is he scary? Why or why not?

3. Dante has intentionally not named the name of Christ in Hell. For the same reason he gave *Inferno* 34 cantos, instead of 33 (the age of Jesus when He died and rose again). Why do you think that might be?

4. Read Isaiah 14:12–15 and discuss Dante's mythology concerning the fall of Satan: his tomb, the land fleeing, part to the north, part to form Mount Purgatory, and the abyss that forms at his head. Tie in the myth of the statue on Crete, and its tears that form the four rivers of Hell. What is Dante wanting to communicate, at the macro level, about the nature of Hell?

5. What is the significance of seeing the stars again?

6. Wrapping it all up, what is the primary lesson Dante wants to teach us about the nature of sin?

ROMAN ROADS CLASSICS
////

Also available from Roman Roads Press:

Inferno: Book One of the Divine Comedy, Dante Alighieri,
a blank verse translation by Joe Carlson

Purgatorio: Book Two of the Divine Comedy, Dante Alighieri,
a blank verse translation by Joe Carlson

Paradiso: Book Three of the Divine Comedy, Dante Alighieri,
a blank verse translation by Joe Carlson

ROMAN ROADS CLASSICS

Praise for the *Inferno: Reader's Guide*

"To accompany his smooth and literate translation of Dante's *Divine Comedy*, Joe Carlson has put together a series of excellent Reader's Guides that provide the necessary historical, literary, philosophical, and theological background. More than that, he provides incisive analysis that draws out the deeper Christian meanings and carefully-worded discussion questions that will challenge students and teachers alike to explore the full dimensions of Dante's great epic. A great resource for homeschooling parents and classical Christian teachers."

—Louis Markos, Professor in English and Scholar in Residence, Houston Baptist University; author of *The Myth Made Fact: Reading Greek and Roman Mythology through Christian Eyes*

Purgatorio: Reader's Guide

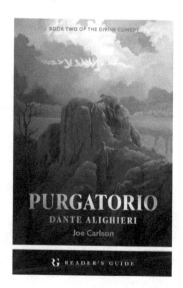

Paradiso: Reader's Guide

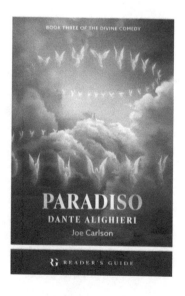

ROMAN ROADS CLASSICS

The Iliad and *The Odyssey* of Homer, a new prose rendering by Wesley Callihan

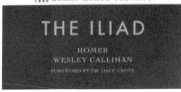